Global Strategy

The *Global Dimensions of Business* series provides authoritative summaries of the latest developments in international business and management.

Books in the series provide:

- focused, topic-based summaries of the key global developments in the different sub-disciplines of business
- an international perspective on the core topics in the curriculum for executive, MBA, and advanced graduate students in business
- strategic and practitioner implications in each topic area
- commentary on emergent and changing trends as well as established knowledge

Selected titles in the series:

Global Strategy by Stephen Tallman
Managing the Global Workforce by Paula Caligiuri, Dave Lepak and Jaime Bonache

Global Strategy

GLOBAL DIMENSIONS OF STRATEGY

Stephen Tallman

Robins School of Business,
University of Richmond

John Wiley & Sons, Ltd.

Published in 2009 by John Wiley & Sons, Ltd

© 2009 Stephen Tallman

Registered office
The Atrium, Southern Gate, Chichester, West Sussex, PO19 8SQ, United Kingdom

For details of our global editorial offices, for customer services and for information about how to apply for permission to reuse the copyright material in this book please see our website at www.wiley.com.

Library of Congress Cataloging-in-Publication Data

A catalogue record for this book is available from the Library of Congress.

A catalogue record for this book is available from the British Library.

ISBN 978-1405-13610-5

Typeset in 10/12.5 Rotis Serif by Aptara Inc., New Delhi, India.
Printed in Great Britain by TJ International Ltd, Padstow, Cornwall, UK.

Dedicated to Marcia and Tess

CONTENTS

LIST OF FIGURES

PREFACE

This book has been in preparation for several years, partly for personal and career issues and partly because the environment of international strategy has been changing so rapidly that freezing a book for publication seemed ever untimely. However, the purpose for which it was originally conceived still seemed relevant in the Autumn of 2008, so I finally pushed it through to completion, even in the midst of perhaps the greatest upheaval in the international economy in 60 years. This purpose is and was to make international strategic issues more immediate and accessible for those studying business strategy, even as the importance of the topic has become ever more apparent. When this project began, there was no international strategic management textbook. In the past few years, several have emerged, but each has been aimed at a different market niche and has used a different approach. This book, too, is intended to bring the topic to a specific audience.

I was teaching both business strategy and international strategy at the time that this book was conceived, mostly to Executive MBA students. I observed several characteristics of this market that gave this book its form. First, the circumscribed schedules of Executive MBA programs seldom leave room for two classes on a topic, and the marginal value of an international strategy course in addition to a business strategy class seemed to be less than what was needed to justify an international elective. Second, EMBA and executive courses seemed to be moving toward short formats, either intensive weeks or half-term classes, particularly for electives. Third, the conditions under which international strategy was being employed were constantly changing and strategic responses were evolving rapidly, so that a course taught from an established text seemed by necessity to be always out of date. At the same time, some underlying issues and dimensions of strategy and strategy-making seemed to be holding up well under trying conditions. In my own teaching, my solution was to use sets of journal articles and cases, backed up by materials from the current news, to teach a strategic management course set in the international environment. However, I found this to be a disjointed and expensive approach, as many articles were long and costly, but often provided only background material or a few key points set in a longer, but not necessarily relevant, article. This led to student resentments over high book fees and lack of direct application of these materials. Cases became outdated or irrelevant, and telling students to "ignore the context" or to imagine that they were in an environment without the internet was not a viable solution.

As a result, I concluded that a relatively short, relatively inexpensive text, focused on the core issues of strategic management and international strategy and presented in the more-or-less standard "strategy process" format was needed. This book is my answer to that concern. It is not long as these things go. It does not contain the many features that bring in costly external materials such as cases or that are meant to provide immediate relevance, but which add to publishing costs and which require constant updating. It also covers the basics of strategic management as well as the important aspects of strategy making and execution in the international context. By keeping both financial and time investments in the core concerns low, this text allows the instructor to supplement the course with journal articles offering the latest really cool but untested ideas, with cases of his or her own choosing and with articles from daily and weekly news outlets or from the web, all without putting counterproductive pressures on the students. Its format allows it to be used either in an elective on international strategy or in a short core course on strategic management that keeps the international aspects in focus throughout. It is short enough to be used in a concentrated executive course and complete enough to be the basis for a term-length course with added materials. At least, these are ways in which I will use it – and I hope that others will find both the approach and the text itself to offer a valuable foundation for an evolving course covering a dynamic set of issues.

CHAPTER 1
Strategy for the Global Marketplace

Strategy in Action

Founded in 1961 by Leonardo del Vecchio, Luxottica is the world's largest eyeglass company and one of the largest and fastest growing companies in Italy.[1] It began as supplier of eyeglass frames to the industry, and was based in the Italian region of Belluno – the center of eyeglass production in Italy. In 1967, Luxottica began to manufacture for its own brand as well as making contract parts and by 1971, it ceased contract production to become a full line manufacturer and retailer. The company then began a program of acquisition of competitors in eyeglass and sunglass manufacturing and marketing, to include Scarrone, an Italian eyeglass distribution company, and culminating in the purchase of struggling RayBan in 1999 from Bausch & Lomb. Luxottica produces eight house brands such as REVO and Arnette and has also procured exclusive licenses for a variety of luxury designer lines such as Bvlgari, Burberry, Chanel, Dolce & Gabbana, Donna Karan, Prada, Versace, and Polo Ralph Lauren – 17 in all. Its wholesale operations cover 130 countries and Luxottica has moved into downstream operations by purchasing Sunglass Hut, the world's largest retailer of sunglasses, and companies such as Pearle Vision and LensCrafters, major eyeglass retailers in the US market, and OPSM and Laubman & Pank in the Asia-Pacific region. It is the leading retailer in North America, China, Australia, New Zealand, and the UK.[2] At the same time, the company has expanded the size and scope of its manufacturing business, with six plants in the Belluno region of Italy, but also two in China for the production of less expensive frames. Luxottica maintains a network of designers and parts producers in Northern Italy, as well as having long-term relationships with production machinery manufacturers for its factories.

Luxottica controls its value-adding process from design to final sale, but hardly does so as a classic hierarchical bureaucracy with tight central control of all operations. Rather, the core company focuses on its established skills – designing and producing a wide variety of high-quality, fashion-conscious frames. Plastic frames are manufactured in plants located in Sedico, Pederobba, and Turin, while metal frames are manufactured in the plants located in Agordo and Rovereto – all in Italy. It makes small metal parts in yet another Italian plant. Leonardo del Vecchio says that "... in-house manufacturing resulted in many process innovations ... when you manufacture in-house, you're forced to improve ...".[3] Its marketing operations manage its own brands, but much of its production is sold under a variety of labels through collaborative relationships with many of the major French and Italian design houses. It distributes through 38 internal branches and 100 independent distributors in 130 countries. Its retail operations provide important, though hardly exclusive, outlets for its production, but continue to be managed independently, with separate brand identities and inventory from both the parent company and from competitors. Luxottica accesses the profits from retail operations and the benefits of direct contact with final customers, while Sunglass Hut and the others can use the superior credit and assets of their large parent in pursuing their rapid expansion plans in many markets around the world. The upstream network of parts design and manufacturing allies also work on nonexclusive bases, offering Luxottica new ideas and skills for certain items, while not saddling the company with capital commitments and workforce concerns in what are important, but peripheral, operations.

While Luxottica uses some very advanced materials and production methods, it offers a very traditional product, with much excess value coming from design and labeling – basic marketing tools. Luxottica is winning through its commitment to modern strategic management, not through having exclusive access to advanced product or process technology, not through monopolistic practices in mature markets or by moving all of its production to low-wage locations. The company taps all of these potential sources of advantage at times, but so do its competitors – who often use the same suppliers and outlets. Rather, it is the global vision of its founder and the combination of efficiency and innovation that arise from its networked organization that seem to free Luxottica to follow untried paths in an old, established industry that make it a success and a model for companies looking for success in the new century.

Globalization

Business strategy as the twenty-first century dawns is global strategy. Much is made of global markets, but competition, innovation, and organization are equally global. This is only a reflection, though, of the convergence of individual tastes for worldwide brands at the expense of local cultural preferences, worldwide political domination by a small number of industrialized and industrializing states and the emergence of several major new (or revived) political and economic players, the increasing strength of international nongovernmental organizations (NGOs), the integration of capital markets worldwide, the increasing ubiquity of communication and information around the world, and the spread of technology to the farthest reaches of the globe. Indeed, the impact of technology, and particularly information and communication technology (ICT), is the other characteristic aspect of twenty-first century business, one which is essential to modern globalization, dependent as it is on constant and immediate communication around the globe. Even as I work on the final draft of this book, the worldwide financial crisis and accompanying fears of a worldwide economic crash emphasize how broadly and quickly both good and bad developments spread. In later chapters, we will see that there is a debate on whether multinational companies are really globalizing, or remaining focused on their home regions. The current situation seems to me to have laid to rest such academic discussions in relation to markets and to the strategies, if not the asset bases, of the companies that compete in them. If the various economic regions of the world crash together, they must rise together – global is here, now.

The companies that are most involved with globalization, whether as practitioners or victims, are those multinational corporations, like Luxottica, that operate – not just sell – in multiple national markets and compete against other firms just like themselves. This book is about strategic management in multinational corporations (MNCs) competing in a technology-enabled and globalizing marketplace. It is about strategic management – indeed, it is organized as a strategy book. But it is also about international businesses and organizations and those aspects of strategy that are unique to companies operating in the international arena

Globalization is a term that is widely used, but with few limits on its possible meanings. I use it in relation to business strategy to describe the increasing integration of national and regional markets and economies and the domination of the world economy by massive multinational firms. As culture, politics, employment, and other aspects of nonbusiness life also become more global, the global strategies of multinational enterprises naturally are of great concern to business, but are of equal interest to governments, NGOs, and people who – individually and collectively – buy from, work for, fear, distrust, desire, court, sue, and otherwise interact with these companies. It seems that concern for global strategy is a particularly timely issue. This volume is intended to provide you with the basic knowledge needed to understand the forces driving international and global strategies, the character of such strategies, and the actions firms take to survive and prosper in the global economy.

A global strategy implies strategic involvement in many regions and nations around the world, but MNCs can also be widely spread without integrating their operations – they can be international, but not global – or they can integrate their operations over a smaller geographical area – they can be regional, not worldwide, in their scope. We shall see that the decision to operate abroad, to internationalize, really is separate from (if closely related to) the decision to integrate these widespread operations, to globalize. Further, we will see that most multinational firms do limit their international presence to certain regions of the world, having regional rather than global strategies, but they still must decide both how many countries they will enter (and how they will do this) and whether they will integrate their value-adding operations across national borders or run each national subsidiary as an essentially independent company. And, even if companies limit their own geographic spread, they are exposed to influences – competitors, technologies, products, money – from other regions and countries to the point that regional physical scope hardly means that the company is not engaged in the global economy.

We will also see that the strategies of MNCs may involve all the activities and operations of these firms. International business studies have long been concerned about the internationalization and globalization of markets; about how MNCs have been able to enter foreign markets with products, skills, and market power developed in their home markets in order to increase their profits and maintain their growth. At the same time, other MNCs have looked to foreign countries as sources of production factors, whether raw materials such as minerals or agricultural products, land, labor or capital to enable them to sell less expensive or more desirable products in their home markets – or in additional foreign countries. More recently, though, recognition has grown that MNCs can also find better products, superior processes, and greater knowledge outside their home country, and that the rapid improvements in ICT in recent years enable them to coordinate multiple dispersed operation centers to create a variety of superior products for multiple dispersed markets at costs that are below those of locating integrated operations in single markets, whether at home or abroad. This technology-enabled complexity has resulted in dramatic changes in business models, in employment, in political pressures, and in strategic management of these modern MNCs – referred to as Metanational,[4] Transnational,[5] or Integrated Global[6] firms. It is not just raw material extraction and foreign sales that drive companies into the international arena any more.

Strategic Management

However, as I said above, this is not a book about international business – it is about the strategies of multinational corporations. It is intended to provide a solid background for a course on multinational strategy but to permit the time and space to supplement these basics with up-to-date materials such as readings, current event discussions, and current case examples of global strategy. In a constantly and rapidly changing environment, this seems to be the only way to retain relevance beyond the very short term. It will be organized around the basic structure of the strategic decision-making process. As such, it will parallel most business strategy or strategic management textbooks and courses.

This is done for two main pedagogical reasons and one personal reason. The latter is that I am a strategy professor as well as an international business professor, and tend to think in strategy terms. The first pedagogical issue is that I want to differentiate this book from the many texts about the environment of international business and the many other texts that focus on international management. This book is about strategy – strategy in the multinational, but strategy nonetheless. The second issue is the potential use for this book. It is intended to be used for a strategy elective, and particularly for executive or executive MBA audiences who are familiar with strategy and the strategy process, so it should be familiar in its organization. It introduces issues of internationalization and globalization within this familiar framework so that managers and prospective managers see how the concerns of international business fit into their strategic decision-making processes, rather than being a separate body of knowledge to be interpreted by the user. I also hope that this format will allow some programs to use this book as the basis, with appropriate supporting material, for a global strategy course that can replace the typical "strategy core course" without compromising students' opportunities to learn and apply general strategy principles and models.

As such, an introduction to business strategy concepts is necessary in order to put the rest of the book in perspective. That is the objective of most of the rest of this introductory chapter. So, let's talk about strategy a bit. First, there are a variety of definitions of just what business strategy and strategic management are. In the simplest sense, business strategy is what businesses do and strategic management is about the planning and execution of activities by which "it" is done. Strategy is about market positioning, about responding to the competition, the environment, and the customer. It is about being good at what we do, being efficient, being unique and innovative, about having better products and processes and more effective managers, about creating detailed plans and responding quickly to changing times.

The Strategy Process

The process of developing a business strategy generally follows a familiar sequence, as we see in Figure 1.1. The *Mission* of the firm is its larger sense of purpose. From an economic perspective, firms

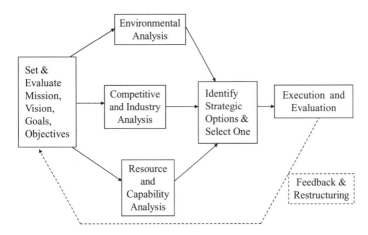

Figure 1.1   The multinational strategy process.

exist to increase the wealth of their owners or shareholders. However, many successful firms have mission statements that are pithier,
more emotionally appealing, more motivating, or that offer broader
perspectives on the role of the firm in society. Jack Welch has been
widely cited for telling GE divisional managers that their goal was to
be first or second in their industry segment or they would be gone.
Komatsu built itself into a global force in the construction equipment
industry with mottoes such as "maru C" or "Encircle Caterpillar", its
main rival and target.[7] We hear about "No. 1 in customer satisfac-
tion", "Quality is job 1" and the like. On the other hand, the Johnson
& Johnson credo talks about customers, workers, and communities
first and leaves profit as a residual – if we do our job right, we will
be profitable.[8]

Conceptually, we see an ongoing, perhaps even intensifying, debate between what have been called the "shareholder" and the
"stakeholder" models of the firm. The shareholder perspective, generally associated with Anglo-American economic models, and often
associated with Chicago school economists such as Milton Friedman,
contends that the only legitimate role of a business is to provide a
maximum return to its owners or shareholders, and that any attempt
by the firm to pursue non-wealth maximizing directions is inherently wrong – if the owners wish to use their money for altruistic
purposes, they should do so themselves rather than having company
management make the decision for them.

On the other hand, stakeholder models propose that other entities and individuals have made investments in most firms, whether financial or in the form of time and effort with deferred compensation, and have a right to some returns from the business. This position has become more established as ownership of most publicly held companies has become dispersed across many individual and institutional investors rather than concentrated in an owner-manager. Many scholars argue that workers and managers typically have a greater commitment to the firm than do the owners, as they are asked to invest in firm-specific skills that make them less valuable in the open market and to accept deferred compensation such as retirement plans and other benefits. Communities, too, are asked to invest in tax relief, infrastructure improvements, worker education, and so forth in the hope of attracting jobs and eventually larger tax bases. Society in general provides the stable political, economic, and social systems that enable firms to operate at a low cost to shareholders, but at a clear cost to taxpayers. These and other stakeholders should receive direct benefits from the firm, even at some expense to equity investors.

While economic theory perhaps should not be presented as an absolute measure of right or wrong, but rather as offering various ways of resolving competing demands, the missions of corporations can become a matter of intense debate over equity, efficiency, short versus long-term benefits, the role of business in society, even the meaning of work to humanity. As part of the debate on these issues within most societies, companies typically can negotiate the course in domestic markets, as managers are part of the society. However, internationalization forces companies to do business in places where the social equilibrium may be much different. While companies in the US can generally open and close facilities, hire and fire workers, and start and end lines of business without legal consequence, these companies find that most other countries are less accepting of what they see as business necessities. European countries tend to see employment and the rights of workers as having a higher priority than corporate profits. Taxation of corporations varies greatly around the world. Companies doing business in China must be more engaged with government agencies than is typical in market economies, including as partners and competitors. In general, most of the world takes a more stakeholder-oriented perspective than does the US, forcing companies to take on much more socially conscious missions than they may pursue in the US – though, of course, social and environmental consciousness is rising in America, too, and activist pressures may work through shareholders to encourage more of a stakeholder orientation, even as laws and regulation offer direct protection much more to shareholders.

At the same time, MNCs based in industrial economies, particularly in the US, are often seen as propping up or aiding foreign governments to the detriment of home-country policies, economics, and individual workers. "Statelessness" of MNCs, implying autonomy of action with no nationalistic concern or even ruthlessness, is a growing concern of many governments and activists even as it offers many benefits to operations and to shareholders. A key part of the mission of any MNC is to define how much it is a home-country firm with international interests, and how much it is a global economic entity with ties to many states, but loyalties only to its owners – and maybe to other direct stakeholders, but not to idealized concepts of citizenship perhaps more appropriate to individuals.

Within its broader mission, a business firm must define a set of *Goals and Objectives*. These are immediate outcomes that management can pursue and against which its performance can be measured. Such goals and objectives should support the mission. From a shareholder perspective, profitability (however measured) and growth (also subject to a variety of measures) tend to be the focus, as ever-increasing profits tend to maximize equity values over time. A currently popular measure that summarizes various measures is the concept of Economic Value Added, which suggests that long-term shareholder value derives from a combination of performance measures. From a stakeholder perspective, these economic goals remain important, but other measures such as the *triple bottom line*, or net performance on economic, social, and environmental measures, are becoming popular. Even firms that may not have a strong initial commitment to noneconomic goals may be forced to consider these other outcomes by activist shareholders, particularly public institutions such as public retirement funds or university portfolio managers. For multinationals, a wider set of goals and objectives to support more social and environmental missions may be strongly encouraged or even required in some countries. In the end, though, if the business firm does not perform well economically, it will be able to do little in other spheres of endeavor.

In general, the approach taken here is that the real objective of business strategy is to generate sustained competitive advantage for the firm. Competitive advantage can be used to create growth in sales, increase market share, expand into new businesses or markets, or to generate greater profits. Different firms may use competitive advantage for different purposes, and any one firm may switch from growth to profit to social objectives over time, but without a source of competitive advantage, none of these outcomes is possible. From a micro-economic perspective, competitive advantage is reflected by the idea of producer surplus. The firm that can either sell at a market price while facing lower costs, or that can produce a unique product that can support a price premium while still attracting adequate demand will generate above-normal profits. From a strategic perspective, competitive advantage occurs when a firm can provide increased value to its customers, whether through low prices or through improved products, and can therefore attain or surpass its competition and its own goals, whether by generating greater than normal profits or by taking customers away from competitors.

However, just having a competitive advantage over other firms in an industry at a particular point in time is generally not adequate to long-term success, so this book will argue for the importance of sustained competitive advantage. As we shall see, the book takes what has been called a resource-based strategy perspective, one which proposes that competitive advantage comes to a firm through its access to unique or firm-specific resources, to include entrepreneurial and managerial capabilities. Sustained advantage comes from the ability to develop new resources and capabilities and to apply them to new markets as the economic and competitive environment changes, competitors copy successful strategies and resources, innovation changes customer options, and so forth. Only by adapting its internal capabilities and accessing new assets, together with expanding its scope for applying these resources, can a firm keep up with the ever-evolving environment of business – a condition that is only exacerbated in the international realm.

In order to pursue its goals and objectives in support of its overall mission, the managers of a firm must understand the *internal and external environments* of the firm. Sometimes referred to as SWOT (Strengths and Weaknesses, Opportunities, and Threats) analysis, this stage of the strategy process requires the identification of the resources and capabilities of the firm as well as the external competitive and contextual environment of the firm. The internal resources of the firm are the key to sustained competitive advantage in the model followed in this book. Most of the assets and capabilities of any firm are needed just to take part in an industry, to stay even with other competitors. However, most firms have certain unique, firm-specific assets and capabilities that are not exactly the same as those of other firms. If these resources can be applied to offer unique value, whether lower prices, better quality, higher performance, or some other preferred characteristic, to customers, the firm theoretically can generate economic rents from the resources – and in a strategic sense, can use these resources to generate competitive advantage. If the resources can be renewed and replaced as the world changes, this becomes a sustained competitive advantage. Of course, if management identifies resources that are weaker than those of the competition, it must find a way to reach competitive parity before seeking advantage, so understanding limitations is as important as knowing where the firm is strong.

Since resources only generate advantage and value when applied in the marketplace, managers must understand their environment. This applies to the larger exogenous context in which the firm operates – the political, economic, legal, social, and cultural environment. Obviously, this aspect of assessment is critical to multinational enterprises, as the dimensions of the international business environment vary from country to country and are also dependent on relationships between countries. While managers in a domestic environment may be able to largely assume the character of their home market, managers in the international realm never have that luxury. The other aspect of the environment that is particularly relevant to a business firm is the competitive environment. Who are our competitors? What are they doing? Where are they beating us and where are we beating them? Can we benchmark their capabilities? Can we match their technology? These and myriad similar questions reveal the opportunities and threats in the industry's competitive environment. In today's world, virtually all firms must consider international threats and opportunities. This is obvious for the case of MNCs, but even domestic firms may face international competition that may be much stronger than, or at least considerably different from, immediate domestic competition. Globalization brings much more uncertainty to environmental analysis.

Once strategic managers understand their resource stock and their environment, they are ready to begin *planning strategies* to pursue the firm's goals and objectives. A viable strategy needs to be congruent with the resource base and suited to the environment, as well as appropriate to the goals and objectives of the firm and internally consistent. A strategy with a bad fit in any of these areas will leave the firm in a long and difficult struggle with little chance for ultimate success. Multinational firms have a wider array of strategic choices, as well as more dispersed and differentiated resource bases and more complex environments, so while the process is similar in any firm, it is likely to be much longer and more complicated in the international environment. It is at this stage that managers must consider expanding into new product lines or new markets, the degree of diversification that they want for the firm, what are core and what peripheral activities, whether they are prepared to pursue acquisitions or alliances in moving ahead, how directly they are willing to challenge their competitors, and a variety of other strategic choices.

Closely tied to the choice of strategy is the *execution of strategy*. On the planning side, execution involves issues of structure and systems to provide the control, coordination, and communication needed to pursue the strategy. However, execution carries over into operations – more strategies fail because they are poorly pursued than because they are badly conceived. Excellence in operating the firm is as important to the firm as excellence in strategic planning. However, as soon as the strategy is put in place and the firm begins operation, new opportunities or new problems are likely to arise and lead the firm in new strategic directions. Henry Mintzberg refers to this as emergent strategy, strategy that develops as the firm operates, as compared to planned strategy that is laid out through the strategic planning process described here.[9] In addition, some parts of any planned strategy will simply not work as unexpected variations or changes in the environment are hit, leaving some aspects of the plan unrealized. A solid plan makes a solid base for the firm's strategy, but flexibility in execution to allow non-viable plans to be dropped and emerging opportunities to be pursued is equally important to strategic success. Again, the complex and evolving international environment is likely to offer multinational firms more and more varied opportunities to develop emergent strategies, making planning for change and considering investments as options rather than commitments critical for long-term success.

Of course, strategic management is a process itself, not just the outcome of a planning process. Even allowing for emergence of new strategic directions is insufficient to a changing environment. Managers must revisit the planning process on a regular, even an ongoing, basis. Success and failure in attaining goals and objectives and pursuing the mission of the firm must be evaluated, nascent strategic directions considered, new developments in the business environment and in the industry's competitive context evaluated, and new plans made. Political, economic, social, and technological environments do not stand still and the firm cannot either.

The Structure of the Book

So, how will all this strategy be integrated with international business concerns into a coherent volume? The next chapter addresses the ideas of mission and objectives in more detail, and shows how, when, and why MNC managers must think much more broadly about these issues than do most managers of domestic firms – even ones that have a thriving export business. Once companies begin to establish operations and locate assets in companies other than their home base, they become subject to new laws and regulations, they must understand new cultures, they can no longer favor one set of workers over another for non-economic reasons, and they must incorporate all these and many other considerations into their reasons for existing and the goals and objectives established to support them.

Chapters 3 and 4 consider issues of the environment or context in which international strategies are applied and international operations conducted by multinational companies. In a typical strategy text, one chapter addressing industry and competitive analysis would be sufficient to cover the external "opportunities and threats" faced by the firm and of concern to the strategic manager. The larger environment gets little or no consideration, because it is treated more or less as the water in which the fish swim – ubiquitous and homogenous, therefore not an explicit concern in most situations. For the multinational, though, the macro-environment is essential. The worldwide economy and various national economies are neither constant nor identical – indeed, one important aspect of international strategy is to reduce the negative effects of economic cycles in individual markets through a portfolio approach. Different polit-ical systems, legal systems, and social structures all impact MNCs in positive and negative ways, and must be given due consideration in developing and pursuing global strategies. This is the topic of Chapter 3.

Chapter 4 addresses classic issues of industry and competitive analysis, but on a cross-national basis. Not only must MNCs be con-cerned with emerging firms in existing markets challenging their strategic positions, but they must be aware of other MNCs, based in other countries, that can suddenly become direct competitors – and very strong ones at that. Modern industry spans the globe, and firms must understand their positions relative to the global competition, as well as their standing in each regional and national market or po-tential market. We will look at both essential strategy approaches to industry analysis and international business and economics models of international markets, changing cultures, and alternative insti-tutions and try to integrate these different perspectives and levels of analysis into a coherent set of ideas – although one which will remain quite complicated!

Chapter 5 looks at the internal situation, the status of core com-petencies, dynamic capabilities, and strategic resources within the firm's boundaries – and its more tentative assets available through alliances, contracts, and other network relationships. This analysis of "strengths and weaknesses" combines with understanding the market and the competition (opportunities and threats) to show management just what it has to work with when it goes up against the competition identified in competitive analysis. Given the overall theoretical pos-ture of the book, understanding resources and capabilities, particu-larly those capable of generating superior performance over time, or sustained competitive advantage, is the essence of strategy. Unique firm-specific resources and capabilities (FSRCs), including hard as-sets, unique knowledge, the capacity for innovation, and capabilities for managing these resources in innovative ways are all part of the firm's resource stocks. MNCs hold resources in many locations and have a need to command and control, coordinate and communicate among and about their stocks of resources even more than most firms. It is one thing to know that our R&D facilities are good at coming up with new ways of applying basic physical principles, and something else to also know that these facilities are spread across, and embedded in, Virginia, Bulgaria, and India.

Chapter 6 considers the standard strategic options of MNCs. While recognizing that every strategy should be unique – after all, they are each based on a unique combination of FSRCs, national markets, products and services, and historical antecedents – we also know that there are generic strategic solutions for every broad situation. Much of the study of business strategy has focused on generic strategies and how these fit with markets and resources, but international management models have given us their own generic approaches to broad problems. I hope to introduce ideas from both directions and to show how these can be supporting, complementary approaches to the essential need for alternative ways of acting. It is one thing to be a cost leader, but something much more to be a global low cost producer, to be a niche player, but to have to decide whether that niche will be specific worldwide consumer groups, or perhaps specific regional groups of national markets, or even specific product lines that appeal to different consumers in different places – it gets complicated!

Chapter 7 looks at the structures of multinational corporations. Strategies are fine and all that, but execution is essential, and creating an organization with the best systems for control, coordination, communication, and all the other activities of management is the first step toward executing strategy efficiently. Again, bringing in the geographical dimension alone makes structuring MNCs considerably more difficult than setting up an organization in a local or national market. Considering that it is about the interactions of competing demands for customer attention, production efficiency, and technological superiority *and* the possibilities of many places for both generating and satisfying these demands, global (even regional) integration makes traditional structures and systems far too simple and static to be real solutions.

Chapter 8 looks at entry strategies. No matter how integrated our strategy or how networked our global organization, each new country must be approached for itself as well as being part of the bigger organizational picture. Political, legal, economic, social, and cultural differences, considered as abstract concepts, color the international environment and are a part of Chapter 3, but they become hard realities when set in a particular national context. Entry strategies (and ongoing strategies for subsidiaries) must give deep consideration to all these location-tied issues as well as considering the various organizational and strategic concerns surrounding every

investment. Why do we want to be in China? How do we access
Vietnamese labor? What is going on in Venezuela? Such concerns
are vital to global strategies, even as they must be answered on the
ground in each region, country, and city.

Chapter 9 shifts gears a bit to look at current issues in global strategy in more detail, picking up on the larger, generic concepts laid
out in earlier chapters to consider developing trends in the global
marketplace. The rise of emerging market economies, whether from
poverty or from political isolation, is changing the face of the international economy while giving MNCs a wide array of new opportunities and challenges to meet, to include new multinational
competitors from these countries. The explosion of information and
communication technology is making global management more
possible than ever, but also means that "24/7" strategic management is rapidly becoming the norm, the minimum for competitive
parity in worldwide business. More than ever, multinational strategy is about knowledge strategy, about moving key know-how from
place to place, rather than moving goods and services around. This
has great potential to make MNCs more efficient, but is also creating
a new set of fundamental problems with the location-bound parts
of the international system – the people and the nations – that will
bedevil MNCs as the world moves forward. Outsourcing, offshoring,
the flat world, the wired world, the integrated world, global terrorism, the end of one history and the start of a new one – companies
and investors, workers and consumers, governments and management all have to deal with these and a variety of other new concepts,
some threatening and some promising and most a bit of both. While
breaking my initial rule of trying to avoid a current events approach
to global strategy, this closing chapter will try to focus on the big
picture, the long range prospects for global strategy in the coming
years and decades.

It really must as the collapse of the world financial system, of
demand in most countries, of credit markets globally have such dramatic strategic implications. Indeed, this crisis ties in with this book
in a way that points to the dynamism and scope of the global economy. When I started seriously on the first draft in 2007, the world
economy was booming, and the big question was just how to sort out
winners and losers. When that draft went to my editor in the summer
of 2008, things didn't look quite so good, but it looked like the rise
of China and India and other emerging markets would offset sudden
slowdowns in North America and Western Europe. As I complete the

final draft, alarmists seem to think that the book may have to be published on clay tablets as the entire world economy implodes in a cloud of bad credit and environmental collapse. However, the current despair is likely no more permanent than the previous euphoria. So let's get to it.

Key Points in the Chapter

1 Globalization of business, in this case, refers to the increasing integration of national and regional markets and economies and the domination of the world economy by massive multinational firms.
2 Multinational corporations (MNCs) are companies with operations, not just sales in multiple countries.
3 Strategic management is the management of processes to create, protect, sustain, renew, and exploit unique firm-specific resources and capabilities in the marketplace to gain sustained competitive advantage. Global strategy is strategy practised by multinational corporations in the rapidly globalizing marketplace of the early twenty-first century.
4 The strategy process is designed to offer a systematic, step-by-step method to bring understanding to what often seems a chaotic situation and to offer a reasoned approach to deciding on a path to sustained advantage.

Notes

1 http://luxottica.com/english/profilo_aziendale/index_keyfacts.html.
2 Ibid.
3 Ibid.
4 Doz, Y.L., Williamson, P., and Santos, J. (2001) *The Metanational*. Boston, MA: Harvard Business School Press.
5 Bartlett, C.A. and Ghoshal, S. (1989) *Managing Across Borders: The Transnational Solution*. Boston, MA: Harvard Business School Press.
6 Porter, M.E. (1986) "Competition in global industries: a conceptual frame-work". In M.E. Porter (ed.) *Competition in Global Industries*. Boston, MA: Harvard Business School Press: 15–60.
7 Bartlett, C.A. and Rangan, U.S. (1985) *Komatsu Limited*. Harvard Business School Case 385-277.
8 Aguilar, F.J. and Bhambri, A. (1983) *Johnson & Johnson (A)*. Harvard Business School Case 384-053.
9 Mintzberg, H. (1978) "Patterns in Strategy Formulation". *Management Science*, 24(9): 934–948.

CHAPTER 2
Global Strategy as a Resource-based Strategy

Strategy in Action

One of the great shocks in the international information technology sector in 2005 was the sudden announcement that a little-known Chinese computer manufacturing outsourcer was buying all of iconic IBM's personal computer business. Of course at the time Lenovo, the acquirer, was the largest computer assembler in China and was IBM's primary supplier of personal computers. In what had rapidly become a commodity business, IBM offered brand value, design, marketing, and access to distribution networks. The margins on personal and laptop computers had long been too small to fund design, parts production (except for processor chips), or assembly in high cost locations in the United States. IBM, under CEO Lou Gerstner, considered the profit potential in their many assets and concluded that their systems capabilities could be combined with the same brand name, reputation, innovation, and so forth to generate much greater profits as a computer services company with manufacturing in specialty items such as servers and super computers, rather than as a broad-based consumer products firm.

Lenovo, on the other hand, had many advantages as a computer maker. First, they were located in China, the "world's workshop", with easy access to relatively low-paid but trained, disciplined, and compliant workers. In addition, they had access to a large and rapidly growing domestic market, where they had been manufacturing since 1990 and the market leader since 1997, besides their contract manufacturing for IBM. At the same time, their offshore supplier status

for a major computer seller gave them insight into the expectations
of the international market about cost, design, capability, and reliability. And, of course, Lenovo bought not just the rights to use
IBM's name and logo until 2010, but access to the business assets
of IBM that already complemented their manufacturing prowess, to
include downstream operations and a headquarters complete with
an experienced CEO, Steve Ward (soon replaced by Bill Amelio), located in the US. While the company was registered in Hong Kong
and the chairman, Yang Yuanqing, was Chinese and located in
Beijing, the president was located in upstate New York. Lenovo understood that a simple competency at assembling computers in an
inexpensive location was neither uniquely inexpensive – after all,
all their competitors had similar access – nor capable of producing
unique products that could command premium prices in world markets. Lenovo had core skills in manufacturing, but so did many
Chinese assembly companies, and these particular skills showed
little sign of generating interesting profits – at least they could not
do so without the array of complementary assets built up over years
by IBM. Interestingly, though, this rather unique arrangement was
quite successful in its first years, and Lenovo quickly dropped the
IBM brand name and became the world's fourth largest computer
maker.[1]

At the same time, IBM hardly withdrew from China. Indeed,
IBM maintains thousands of employees and a large market presence in China, as well as one of its international research labs.
IBM's resources simply did not require a hardware base to reach the
world's consumers. The PC business had lost its luster at the product
level. IBM's weaknesses in production were irrelevant if they simply stopped selling commodity computers and used their reputation,
brand, networks of customers, and global spread to invest in the
higher margins of global technical service provision – where they
could make a profitable business.

Indeed, both firms were highly successful until the current downturn, and even now neither is in desperate straits. Lenovo has found
that low costs only put them head to head with strong competitors. The technology sector has slowed, but Lenovo's sudden movement onto the world technology stage has certainly kept the market
more competitive, and its strong position in its rapidly growing and
modernizing home market should give it an advantage in addition
to its basic manufacturing and assembly operations. Lenovo has

operations in 60 countries and core management and technology development in the US, Japan, and China.[2] Even its own brand, brought into use in 2007 even before the IBM license ran out, is seen as a strong resource. On the other side, IBM seems to have made the most of its refocusing to become a solutions company, with a focus on software and systems more than hardware. It has established research labs in China and India, together with six other countries, and is a major supplier of IT consulting and outsourcing management. IBM's unique capabilities for managing technology systems on a massive scale give it a strong position in an equally competitive market. In both cases, focusing on firm-specific unique competences have led to international success, where only a few years earlier, with the commodity PC business hanging around IBM's corporate neck like an albatross, both firms struggled – IBM to compete with lower cost computer makers and Lenovo (then Legend) to break out of its Chinese local market.

As we discussed in the previous chapter, the first step in developing a business strategy is to identify the goals and objectives of that strategy that support the overall mission of the firm, satisfy the demands of investors, and fit with the needs of customers and the possibilities of the firm's resource stocks. Likewise, strategy for a multinational firm is ultimately intended to generate sustained competitive advantage, but in an international or global marketplace.

The Objectives of Business Strategies

The general purpose of business strategies is to acquire, exploit, and defend unique resources and capabilities for the firm in order to create and sustain competitive advantage in the marketplace – find what you are uniquely good at and pursue it. Firms that possess such unique capabilities have the potential to either reduce costs or produce unique products and thereby to increase sales, market share, and size, to generate greater than usual profits, and to create increased economic value for shareholders and other stakeholders. In order to accomplish these economic goals, firms must not just *have* unique assets, though, they must also *apply* these assets in the marketplace to generate products that offer unique value to their customers, whether lower prices, unique capabilities, or some combination of these two concerns. A hoard of secret, but untapped, abilities is of little value. And, finally, firms with unique and valuable assets must also protect these assets from imitation or misappropriation by competitors. A resource or capability shared by all is not a source of economic profits.

While all business strategies are concerned with maintaining and exploiting resources and capabilities to gain sustained competitive advantage, just how this competitive advantage is translated into economic value may vary considerably across strategies. Theory says that unique assets earn "rents", or excess economic returns in the marketplace, because the owners of these unique assets can price outputs based on them according to monopoly pricing models. Thus, if a firm owned all of the world's oil production, it could price for maximum profits, earning considerably more (while producing less) than would a large number of firms in a competitive market. Of course, many producers working together – a cartel such as OPEC in this case – can effectively function to claim increased shares of consumer surplus for the group.

Multinational resource-based strategy in today's world focuses on knowledge resources – routines, capabilities, competencies – that typically may be unique, but that are contestable. That is, other firms either have or can develop similar capabilities given adequate incentives, so that the market is in a state of monopolistic competition.[3] Firms offer differentiated, but not completely unique, products and earn some rents, but these are restricted by indirect or potential competition. Thus, Toyota sells Toyotas and General Motors cannot. However, if Toyota's hybrid models become popular enough, GM and other makers will enter that market segment and drive down Toyota's profits. Rents are most easily comprehended as excess profits – profits in excess of fair market returns – earned by firms that possess unique resources. However, firms can use lower costs due to unique processes to lower prices and increase market share, or price products with unique characteristics at close to market levels and drive sales and share up dramatically. Over time, firms may seek growth in market share initially, then maintain or increase prices in the face of lower costs due to economies of scale or learning effects to increase profits. In the long run, maximizing the wealth of shareholders and the benefits of other stakeholders are the main objectives of business firms, but at any given time competitive advantage may be used for different specific purposes.

The Objectives of *Multinational* Business Strategies

Beyond the essential objective of increased economic value, what forces drive firms to look to international expansion as a strategic move? These forces seem to come from sources both external and internal to the firm. Because the study of multinational firms evolved from the study of international trade, the usual focus has been on drivers of direct investment, though these considerations lie behind international involvements of all sorts. One list of the reasons for international investment, used in whole or part by various scholars over the years, includes the following objectives:[4]

- The search for new markets to exploit existing competencies – Scottish Power runs electric utilities in the United States because it has developed strong skills at managing such facilities that can be applied beyond the borders of Scotland.
- The search for new resources, both natural endowments and those developed by local industry – BP continues to struggle with arbitrary, even illegal, behavior on the part of its Russian partner because that is where the oil is.
- Production-efficiency seeking through economies of scale on regional or global bases – most microprocessor chips (besides Intel's) are made by "chip foundries" with large-scale production and the ability to ship anywhere in the world.
- Technology seeking in countries or localities that have unique product or process development – IT companies from around the world, including India and other emerging markets, maintain operations in Silicon Valley to stay in touch with the latest technology.
- The search for lower risk, both through portfolio effects and by reducing uncertainties through direct involvement – many firms with strong bases in one or more of the traditional Industrial Triad region are looking to emerging markets to find a new place on the business life cycle.
- Countering competition from other multinational firms – the American auto industry, consumer electronics industry, machine tool industry, and others suffered when they tried to defend domestic market positions against Japanese rivals that were able

to subsidize their entry strategies with strong positions in other markets.

From a capabilities-oriented strategic perspective, though, these six points collapse into three main objectives: to leverage existing capabilities in new or larger markets, to acquire or build new resources and capabilities in new places, and to reduce uncertainty and risks from a variety of sources.

In deciding how to find, protect, and apply their unique assets internationally, multinational firms must make two key strategic decisions about the international marketplace. The first is the scope of their international operations (internationalization), which here refers to the choice of how widely to disperse their activities across international locations. The second is their desired degree of cross-national integration or consolidation of operations (globalization or regionalization), which is defined here as the choice of how much to consolidate international markets and operations into a single worldwide strategic entity. Some authors feel that as relatively few companies are actually present in worldwide markets, most preferring to invest primarily in their home regional markets, so consolidation regionally is more relevant to current multinational strategies.[5] Whether regionalization is but a step on the way toward global consolidation or is the end result for most firms, the issue of consolidating and coordinating across various foreign markets remains independent of the drive to spread into new markets.

Resource strategies and multinational strategies work together to generate competitive advantage. Internationalization and integration offer opportunities *to exploit existing resources and capabilities*, both those related to generating superior goods or services and those related to managing the organization. Moving into new markets exploits investments in fixed assets such as brands and technology. Exporting from home markets increases economies of scale in existing plants, while consolidation of multiple national markets regionally (or even across regions) permits the development of large production facilities for regional or world markets – and also permits both the wider exploitation of intellectual property investment and the consolidation of overhead activities in regional or global headquarters facilities. Superior managerial capabilities are also emphasized through internationalization and globalization, as coordinating more and more widespread operations raises constant challenges, and integrating these operations into a single operation, dispersed but responsive, is tremendously demanding. Just as the skills of a Tiger Woods show to best advantage on difficult golf courses, so the challenges of multiproduct multinational competition benefit the most skilled management more than do less complex settings.

Likewise, internationalization and consolidation offer opportunities *to build new resources and capabilities*. Internationalization brings the firm into multiple varied locations where new resources, new ways of operating, new market ideas, and new products can be found and must be tried. Participation in these many markets, particularly through subsidiaries and joint ventures, will give the multinational access not just to new opportunities for exercising its existing capabilities, but to new capabilities that can be internalized, made available to the worldwide firm, and applied in distant local markets, where these new ideas can offer a level of differentiation not available to local competitors. Managing this global organizational learning, as well as directing and coordinating the movement of real goods among subsidiaries around the world, offers considerable opportunities for building organizational capabilities at corporate management. Firms can work themselves into difficulties with excessively fast or broad internationalization, but empirical evidence suggests that experience with increasing international scope and experience with increasing global (or regional) integration leads to success in yet further internationalization and globalization and to superior economic performance.[6]

Internationalization can reduce risks *to protect resources and capabilities* by allowing the multinational firm to spread itself across a variety of regions and countries, seeking markets that are out of phase economically in order to stabilize revenues and earnings. While exposing them to the vagaries of currency exchange rates, internationalization does allow firms to operate in a variety of currencies, and integration across markets does permit them to organize their operations to arbitrage across markets, hedging against economic and financial ups and downs. Thus, even as manufacturing operations from around the world are shifting to China on a large scale, foresighted companies are already looking for the next location for labor productivity when China's wages begin to rise. Business risks can be minimized by operating in the home markets of major competitors, by taking advantage of lower cost, more productive manufacturing sites, managing directly downstream operations in critical markets, and using different markets to support or subsidize each other.[7] Companies have been shown to chase each other around the world in a game of strategic "follow the leader" to prevent a competitor from gaining an advantage in one market that might possibly be exploited in another.[8]

So, if the strategic objectives of firms are to build, protect, and exploit resources and capabilities in order to create sustainable advantage and superior performance, we see that multinational strategy is a valuable tool. Internationalizing into new markets and tying these markets together with the most efficient production offer great opportunities for generating stable profits from the firm's current resources over a broad set of markets. At the same time, building the multinational firm's resource base to compete strongly for future profits is greatly helped by internationalization – new products and ideas come from new and varied locations and new managerial competencies develop from controlling and coordinating many operations in many locations. All these assets and skills applied to assorted markets around the world provide great chances to sustain competitive advantage compared to less multinational competitors. The next sections expand on these ideas in some detail.

Leveraging resources and capabilities: the search for international markets

The primary driver of international expansion in most models of multinational enterprise is the desire to access new, more, and/or larger markets. Classically, firms are said to expand in their own domestic markets until they reach a stable market share in their primary product range. This can be a profitable position for a firm, but pressures for continued growth come constantly and from two primary directions. First, there are the financial markets. Investors seem to appreciate not just profits but growing profits – or at least the promise of growth potential. Growth in revenues, consolidation of markets, reduced competition, and access to new customers all suggest the potential for long-term growing profitability. As increasing the wealth of shareholders (and the benefits to other stakeholders, too) is related in part to size, firms will look to new products and new markets as old product markets are satisfied and become more competitive. And, of course, managers tend to gain disproportionately from running larger firms and have long been seen to pursue growth even when profitability might be higher with a more focused organization.

Second, increasing internationalization is both a way to leverage existing power and to gain new market power by increasing size and as a way to exploit existing power in a wider market.[9] For manufacturing firms based in smaller markets, exports allow plants to operate closer to minimum efficient scale than would domestic sales alone. Further, internationalization of activities provides an effective means of applying existing investments in knowledge resources to a larger market.[10] With an efficient transmission mechanism, international expansion provides increasing economies of scope in applying the unique, firm-specific resources and capabilities of the firm. Any slack resources encourage growth. Edith Penrose, in her *Theory of the Growth of the Firm*, sees the firm made up of a mix of assets and capabilities which are somewhat "lumpy".[11] That is, when a new asset is acquired – a new plant, a new technology, a new management team – it is seldom used fully from the beginning, and excess capacity is a drag on efficiency and profitability. As new and old resources are combined to generate products, increased production is limited finally when some key resource is fully employed – but this leaves slack in other parts of the resource base. In order to employ these assets fully, the firm will expand its markets and product ranges, and invest in added supplies of the necessary resources, which are not likely to exactly match needs, leading to new imbalances and further expansion abroad. This is particularly true of knowledge resources, which are not consumed – indeed are enhanced – with use, and of the management capabilities for directing complex, dispersed firms, which are built up as they are applied and adapted and combined with new approaches discovered in international operations by the MNE organization.

Expansion of American manufacturing into Europe and Japan in the post-World War II era was largely driven by the sense that US firms could apply their same skills and resources in these foreign markets. Deprived consumers would want American goods, or at the least goods that could be produced with the same resources and

a bit of ingenuity, allowing American companies to profit greatly
from their investments in technologies, brands, and so forth. Many
highly internationalized firms went abroad initially thinking that
"if it sells at home, it will have to sell in ...". Of course, this was
and is not always the case, but still larger markets drew firms into
exporting, licensing to foreign partners, and investing in foreign
production.

Many advantages accrue to firms that can access international
markets. The economic pre-eminence of the United States after
World War II made international expansion as a search for customers easy to understand, leading to conceptual models such as
Vernon's International Product Life Cycle.[12] This model proposes
that new products will be developed, made, and sold first in the US,
then in the other industrial states (Western Europe at the time), and
finally in the developing world. Over time, though, the movement of
product innovation to new items, standardization of manufacturing,
and market maturity in the industrial world will shift sales and production first to Europe, then to the developing world. Net exports
will shift away from the US and industrial world to the developing
countries over time, as mature markets offer only replacement demand and growth is focused in the emerging economies. This model
was highly descriptive of the world economic situation in the 1950s
and 1960s, but even Ray Vernon recognized its problems as the rest
of the world began to catch up with the US. Today, innovation comes
from many locations, particularly across the industrial world, production moves rapidly to low cost but competent locations through
outsourcing, and demand around the world is rapidly homogeniz-
ing. Firms focus on manufacturing in China and developing IT skills
in India, not to provide outdated products in response to slowly
growing markets in those countries, but as suppliers to demanding
markets in the industrial world and exploding demand locally for
the hottest technologies.

Sumantra Ghoshal pointed to the strategic focus on increased
efficiency.[13] Applying existing sets of assets and capabilities to a
larger customer base allows multinational firms to earn greater returns on their investments in processes and products than they can
manage in their home markets alone – even in large markets such as
the United States. Companies find that they gain efficiency and become more competitive by expanding into new markets and/or new
product lines. Certain of these firms eventually discover that they

still have latent efficiencies and competitive benefits when they have conquered their share of the home market. Of course, the point at which this happens is very dependent on the size of the home market and on the industry. Firms from small countries often become multinationals while still quite small. In larger home markets, traditional industries can accommodate fairly large firms before companies begin to look abroad, while technology-intensive companies often look for international customers when they are formed[14] – consider the burgeoning Internet-based scene as an example. Whatever the point in their lives that companies begin to look to international markets, they can gain economies of scale by producing for regional or global markets, and economies of scope for fixed investments in technology, brands, or distribution by applying these resources to broader markets. When such economies are of particular relevance to an industry, firms are driven to integrate their operations across markets to take maximum advantage of efficiency benefits,[15] although the degree of integration that provides maximum benefit varies from industry to industry and from activity to activity.[16]

Even in these days of burgeoning use of offshore production platforms, overseas production is often tied to the search for new markets, as economic, social, and consumer demands make exports and licensing less competitive in foreign markets. China may offer inexpensive manufacturing for Wal-Mart in the US, but it also offers a huge market for Wal-Mart and others in China itself. Production in and for the local foreign market, the host market, may limit economies of scale, but does permit close adaptation to local demand patterns. Production for regional markets, such as North America or Western Europe, permits plants to be larger than would be efficient for single national markets, yet somewhat adaptable, and also takes advantage of cross-selling within regional trading blocs. For instance, when Electrolux of Sweden bought Zanussi of Italy, it consolidated production of various types and models of household appliances, keeping plants in various countries of Western Europe open, but shifting production so that each plant could specialize in a limited range of products for the entire regional market. MNCs can gain efficiencies through centralized international production, and can also benefit from lower factor costs and possibly from superior process technology. Market-based internationalization begins to improve efficiency in the home country, but becomes the basis for improved efficiency, superior technology, and improved quality through a global perspective on all phases of the value chain, not just sales. The organization can learn and innovate as it adapts to a variety of new environments.[17]

While some recent studies have sought to raise doubts about the often proposed, but less than fully proven, connection between multinationalism and firm performance,[18] others continue to support this relationship. The overall evidence seems to suggest that traditional economies of scale in production tie to the overall size of markets and to the production technologies in use. Minimum efficient scale can be reached in larger domestic markets, or by exporting from over-sized home-based plants. Simple production economies may be satisfied by exports – but actually selling products in foreign markets may be greatly assisted by local downstream operations. More to the point, economies in the application of firm-specific knowledge resources and management capabilities seem to be very much tied to multinational expansion and integration. What have been called economies of scope (wider ranges of products and markets) or enterprise-level economies of scale (as opposed to traditional plant-level scale economies) are related to finding the maximum number of opportunities to apply the knowhow that is the ultimate source of sustained competitive advantage. Given the public-good nature of knowledge – it is not used up in application (indeed, probably increases as it is applied in different circumstances) – and that combination with locally specialized knowledge adds value in specific markets, it would seem that the information-age multinational firm will gain value by extending its hard-won competencies to gain competitive advantage in as many markets as possible.

As an example, we see Microsoft investing in significant software development in China, even as it faces massive difficulties in defending its intellectual property in that same market. Local value-adding activities offer both inexpensive software engineering and encouragement to the local authorities to continue to rein in intellectual property fraud. Most importantly, though, even in the face of challenges to its immediate revenue potential in East and Southeast Asia, Microsoft (and its competitors) are not avoiding or exiting markets. Threats of loss of proprietary resources have in the past led firms to exit markets – Coca-Cola from India, IBM from Mexico, for instance. Today, though, the need to gather returns from massive investment in new products forces companies like Microsoft to compete everywhere. Their sales may be limited in China, but their products (or at least pirated versions of their products) are ubiquitous. The hope is that as China becomes wealthier, and as local intellectual property production increases, regulation and the market will shift to legitimate versions and the company will see rapid growth in profits in the Chinese market.

Building resources and capabilities: the international search for innovation

Of course, Microsoft is also developing its products and its production capacity in China. Large numbers of well-trained engineers offer both lower development costs and possible new ideas from a unique language and culture. Microsoft and other software firms – not to mention many companies in other industries – expect to create new products and new capabilities for generating products in locations such as China, India, Eastern Europe and other emerging markets by bringing new populations and new ideas into their operations.

Natural resource companies have become multinational through seeking assets rather than markets, and other firms have moved abroad to service home markets from less expensive locations or have recognized that they could access new resources and capabilities in locations where they originally sought new markets. For centuries, companies in the natural resource extracting industries (mining, agriculture, wood products, and so forth) have looked to overseas sources of supply, not so much to enter foreign markets as to continue to service home customers. Of course, once established in a foreign country, companies often discover local demand for their products, as well as the ability to compete in other international markets. Thus, the major oil companies entered the Middle East in search of large, easily extracted, and inexpensive supplies of crude oil to supply customers in their respective home markets. However, they quickly found that once established in Arabia, BP and Royal Dutch/Shell could sell into North America or Asia, and Exxon or Mobil into Europe as easily as they could access their home markets, and they created a global market for petroleum products. So, the imperative to find newer, larger, less expensive or more accessible natural resources has long driven firms to look to foreign markets. While natural resource industries are a shrinking portion of industrial capacity in today's marketplace, they still hold crucial roles, and still operate internationally to find and exploit such resources.

A second resource, or production factor, driver of international expansion is the need for inexpensive, productive labor. The earliest theories of international trade looked to the distribution of workers and worker skills as important to national comparative advantage and to the benefits of trade. Early models of direct foreign investment treated this as an alternative to trade by which capital could move across borders to seek low cost, underemployed labor, rather than countries trading capital and labor-intensive goods. Even as labor productivity has tended to converge across the industrial world, the entry of big emerging markets into the world's market economy has been encouraged and funded by demand for their relatively inexpensive, but adequately skilled, workers. We will examine outsourcing more closely in a later chapter, but for now we can say that whether seeking underemployed mathematicians in Eastern Europe, farmers migrating to factories to manufacture cheap consumer goods in China, or the brightest IT graduates in India, multinational firms are busily using foreign workers to reduce the costs of their products sold in the advanced nations. Of course, as payments and investments flow into these countries to pay for production, this labor is becoming more expensive, and their new wealth is attracting investment targeted at their potential markets, but the cycle began and is largely supported today by the "global workshop" of the emerging world.

However, asset-seeking investment has been transformed in the modern era beyond the search for location-based comparative advantages tied to natural resources and inexpensive labor to a search for the best, most competitive worldwide source of new skills and knowledge as embodied, for instance, in Porter's model of created advantage in national clusters.[19] The multinational firm becomes a mechanism for transmitting knowledge rather than intermediate goods. The diversity of environments in which multinationals operate provides greater opportunity to gain unique skills and to find the numbers of skilled workers that burgeoning technology demands. The integrated global companies in today's economy seek knowledge as much as hard assets, and are increasingly willing to develop their businesses around what they see as "sticky knowledge", maintaining and developing the knowledge base in its intellectual home ground and transmitting codified or embodied bits of knowledge rather than trying to transplant the underlying knowhow. Empirical studies of ICT outsourcing are consistently finding that labor costs are much less important than are indicators of a supply of highly skilled workers – educational levels, to include those for women, higher salaries for skilled workers, number of universities. Filling needs for knowledge workers that simply cannot be found at home is more and more the objective of asset-seeking investment.

Empirical studies suggest that relatively few firms are very good at actually accessing, internalizing, and spreading technology from foreign locations either back to the home country or around the world. Doz's Metanational firm, focused on gathering innovation from around the world and redistributing it to global markets, is an ideal type with notably few real world examples.[20] However, individual firms or individual businesses within firms do manage this feat, and gain by it. Hewlett Packard as far back as 1996 had more than 10% of its global product divisions headquartered (and operating their R&D facilities) in countries other than the United States. Other corporations have recognized that when they discover superior product or process technologies, they are often better building divisions in the originating location than trying to relocate the operations back to the home country – as would be recommended by Porter's diamond of comparative advantage, in which the local conditions that stimulate superior firms and products in a particular business segment cannot be replicated elsewhere.[21] It may be that research seeking to identify the movement of technology is missing the international locating of new product development and related new directions of internal product flows. Research does suggest that most firms still do most of their R&D spending in the home country, but such input measures often miss the strengths of highly focused research in specialized foreign facilities. The best evidence is that multinationals can find and exploit superior resources and capabilities around the world, but are only beginning to understand how to do this effectively. It may be that the organizational capabilities and routines for both moving knowhow and for controlling widespread product bases are the most difficult, and potentially most rewarding, competencies needed for effective knowledge-seeking multinational strategies.

Protecting resources and capabilities – international risk reduction objectives

Risk, or factors creating variability in returns, is an unavoidable aspect of doing business. Multinational firms face what is sometimes a stark choice in choosing appropriate risk–return goals. Returns from exploiting the firm's resources and capabilities in a larger international marketplace are potentially much greater than those available in a smaller home market. Likewise, unique assets collected through international forays into research and development or manufacturing can offer advantages in cost savings or productivity increases. At the same time, making these potential benefits real can involve dramatically increased risks, particularly for less internationally experienced firms. Manufacturing in China is becoming the norm for companies competing in developed markets in a variety of industries, but many a company has found that profitability can be difficult to find in the unfamiliar Chinese market. These risks include business risks – working with unfamiliar partners, the possibility that new markets won't respond to the company's products, the possibility that finances will turn out badly – but also risks tied to location, to differences in government, laws and regulations, culture, economic development, and technological development.

Firms diversify into new products and new markets to reduce their reliance on one set of customers for one line of goods or services for their entire revenue stream. Multinational strategies can figure prominently in strategies to reduce risks. From a macroeconomic perspective, different national and regional markets tend to show different business cycles – though the latest downturn in response to rocketing oil prices and shortages of credit in 2008 seems to be spreading quickly to all markets. The single-nation firm must work within the business cycle of its home market, while the multinational can offset weak demand in one location with strong in another. Other macro, but noneconomic, risks can also be reduced. The effects of political or social processes can be alleviated. For instance, we see companies with environmental pollution problems locating overseas in search of easier regulatory regimes for their production operations than they can find in the European Union or in the United States. And finally, basic business risks can also be reduced. The possibility of competitors lurking abroad to threaten home markets, the danger of relying on too small a customer base, the desire to find more reliable and less expensive sources of inputs – all are helped by the wider horizons of global strategy.

Early studies suggested that multinationals reduced their overall risk and that financial markets, at least in the US, recognized this benefit, as valuations of internationally diversified firms tended to be higher than those of matched samples of domestic firms.[22] This would reflect a portfolio effect as multiple product markets stabilized cash flows and earnings over time to reduce overall risk. More recent empirical work, though, suggests that this benefit has been offset by exposure to the vagaries of exchange rates and interest rates.[23] Indeed, relatively few large firms in the industrialized world do not have a degree of international exposure, though most tend to focus in their home regions and still have far less than [a quarter] of their sales outside their home countries, so past differences in exposure to international markets may be shrinking among major multinational firms. Rugman's work on regionalism suggests that most MNCs do most of their business in their home regions, which tend to have closely integrated economies.[24] This minimizes portfolio effects and tends to equalize MNCs, not provide advantage to one against another, but can still offer some benefit as compared to purely domestic firms. Other studies do suggest that firms tend to emphasize either product diversification or international diversification – the number of companies that operate in a wide range of industries over a broad swathe of countries is quite small.[25]

Of course, portfolio strategies require each investment to be independent of the others, and as firms begin more and more to integrate their operations and markets worldwide, this benefit may be lost. Labor unrest in China – or a sudden revaluation in the yuan – will not just affect Chinese companies or companies selling in the Chinese market, but will create production problems for many manufacturing multinationals, most of which have at least some (and often many) of their production operations in China. The economic slowdown in the US market in 2008 is spreading rapidly as it puts pressure on economies of scale for facilities producing for worldwide markets. Integration of markets across the developed world of the Industrial Triad regions has driven multinational firms to look into large emerging markets for millions, even billions, of potential new customers engaged in economic development that is still out of phase with the industrial nations. In the early and mid 1990s, rapid growth among the "Asian Tiger" nations more or less required companies and investors to be in developing Asia. The sudden onset of the Asian currency crisis in 1997, beginning with the collapse of the Thai baht and eventually killing the economies of all developing Asia outside of China, offered considerable opportunity to firms with ongoing strength in the Industrial Triad while bringing considerable pain to those over-committed to the high growth sector of Asia. The last 10 years, though, have resurrected the fortunes of developing Asia, brought first growth and then problems to Latin America, seen the gradual development of a larger European market, and finally the gradual, but continuing (and long-awaited) slide of the US dollar. While regional integration seems to be developing, MNEs can still arbitrage across regional boundaries to reduce the risk of being caught in a stagnant or falling economy. Of course, global concerns such as increasing energy costs affect all markets, though not necessarily equally, and can lead to sudden reevaluations of geographical diversification strategies.

Proving the straightforward portfolio risk-reduction benefits of international diversification has proven difficult – the complexity of the international environment and the growing integration of multinational operations make pure financial risk strategies hard to manage. Most studies focus only on the internationalization of sales or of assets related to market-seeking strategies, so real portfolio effects may be difficult to demonstrate. However, as more and more firms from around the world do move into international markets, the issue is less and less one of offering a superior risk profile to domestic competitors, and more and more one of just keeping level with competing multinationals. Also, the risks of getting caught in price wars with more widely dispersed competitors, as Hamel and Prahalad described for US consumer electronics firms trying to fight off the penetration by Japanese competitors into the American market,[26] or of failing to minimize costs, as is the driving force behind business process offshoring to India, or of missing out on novel products and technologies, as happened with most American communication companies in the development of the mobile telephone, suggest that reducing business risks is more relevant to multinational presence than is simply reducing the variance of corporate profits in the short term.

SUMMARY

The objectives of multinational strategies are much the same as those of any strategy in the larger sense – to build, protect, and exploit unique resources to establish sustained competitive advantage and maximize economic value in the long term. Having an international scope of operations and then integrating these operations on a regional or global basis can be of great advantage in seeking these objectives. Of course, managing a broad geographic scope of operations with complex integration needs is a difficult management challenge. Multinational strategies are not guarantees of success by any means, and any shortage of strategic resources, strategic insight, or worldwide execution can be magnified as quickly as corresponding strengths are by a global approach. The rest of the book is dedicated to showing how multinational firms can go about strategic analysis, strategy selection, and strategy execution in order to best emphasize their strengths and circumvent their limitations in facing the challenges and reaping the rewards of global markets.

This broad definition of the relevant market in comparison to domestic firms does have implications that, in degree if not always in character, are profound. Assets may come from anywhere on the globe, with natural resources unevenly distributed, differing labor costs and competencies, and local institutions varying dramatically from country to country. Resources and capabilities must be protected from many more competitors and from changing conditions country to country that may render rent-generating assets from one market useless or even counterproductive in another. Markets are often protected by law and regulation, shipping can become a significant cost, particularly as energy prices climb, technologies may be incompatible, brand names or product features may not be desirable in foreign markets, or cultural differences may make a product less attractive or even undesirable to consumers. Building, maintaining, and exploiting assets and capabilities are all more challenging internationally – though the rewards to gaining competitive advantage can be much greater in worldwide markets. On the other hand, international markets can provide opportunities to diversify financial and business risks, amortize fixed costs and resource investments over wider customer bases, and cut costs through both scale benefits and foreign production without necessarily hurting the value of the product.

Key Points in the Chapter

1 Key strategic goals include assembling, protecting, and exploiting unique firm-specific resources and capabilities.
2 Key strategic goals of international strategies include geographic scope or degree of internationalization and transnational integration of operations or degree of globalization.
3 MNCs can access resources from many locations around the world in assembling their asset bases and develop skills in managing complex operations as they pull together the activities in multiple locations.
4 MNCs have larger markets in which to exploit their resources and capabilities than do similar domestic firms, improving their potential returns on investment in building these assets.
5 MNCs can reduce their financial risk profiles through international portfolio effects, their country risks by spreading their operations across multiple political entities, and their business risks by increasing their opportunities to access resources and markets and to challenge competitors outside their home markets.

Notes

1 http://en.wikipedia.org/wiki/ Lenovo#History.
2 http://www.lenovo.com/lenovo/ US/en/our_company.html.
3 Chamberlin, E.H. (1933) *The Theory of Monopolistic Competition*. Cambridge, MA: Harvard University Press.
4 Robock, S. and Simmonds, K. (1989) *International Business and Multinational Enterprise*. Homeward, IL: Irwin.
5 Rugman, A.M. and Verbeke, A. (2004) "A Perspective on Regional and Global Strategies of Multinational Enterprises", *Journal of International Business Studies*, 35(1): 3–18.
6 Yip, G.S. (2003) *Total Global Strategy II*. Upper Saddle River, NJ: Pearson Education.
7 Hamel, G. and Prahalad, C.K. (1985) "Do You Really Have a Global Strategy?", *Harvard Business Review*, July–Aug: 139–148.
8 Knickerbocker, F.T. (1974) *Oligopolistic Reaction and Multinational Enterprise*. Cambridge, MA: Harvard Business School Division of Research.

9 Vernon, R. (1966) "International Investment and International Trade in the Product Cycle", *Quarterly Journal of Economics,* 80: 90–207; Stopford, J.W. and Wells, L.T. (1971) *Strategy and Structure of the Multinational Enterprise.* New York: Basic Books.
10 Buckley, P. and Casson, M. (1976) *The Future of the Multinational Enterprise.* London: MacMillan.
11 Penrose, E. (1959) *The Theory of the Growth of the Firm.* New York: John Wiley & Sons, Inc.
12 Vernon, R., n. 9 above.
13 Ghoshal S. (1987) "Global Strategy: An Organizing Framework", *Strategic Management Journal,* 8: 425–440.
14 Oviatt, B.M. and McDougall, P.P. (1995) "Global Start-Ups: Entrepreneurs on a Worldwide Stage", *Academy of Management Executive,* 9: 30–44.
15 Kobrin, S. (1991) "An Empirical Analysis of the Determinants of Global Integration", *Strategic Management Journal,* 12(SI).
16 Prahalad, C.K. and Doz, Y.L. (1987) *The Multinational Mission.* New York: The Free Press.
17 Ghoshal, S., n. 13 above.
18 Hennart, J.-F. (2007) "The Theoretical Rationale for a Multinationality-Performance Relationship", *Management International Review,* 47: 423–452.
19 Porter, M.E. (1990) *The Competitive Advantage of Nations.* New York: The Free Press.
20 Doz, Y.L., Williamson, P., and Santos, J. (2001) *The Metanational.* Boston: Harvard Business School Press.
21 Porter, M.E., 1990, n. 19 above.
22 Agmon, T. and Lessard, D.R. (1977) "Investor Recognition of Corporate International Diversification", *Journal of Finance,* 32: 1049–1055.
23 Reeb, D.M., Kwok, C.Y., and Baek, H.Y. (1998) "Systematic Risk of the Multinational Corporation", *Journal of International Business Studies,* 29: 263–280.
24 Rugman, A.M. and Verbeke, A., n. 5 above.
25 Wiersema, M.F. and Bowen, H.P. (2008) "Corporate Diversification: The Impact of Foreign Competition, Industry Globalization, and Product Diversification", *Strategic Management Journal,* 29: 115–132.
26 Hamel, G. and Prahalad, C.K., n. 7 above.

CHAPTER 3

The Global Strategy Environment

Strategy in Action

International business found a sudden prominence in US Presidential politics in the spring of 2004, when John Kerry denounced national policies that provided tax breaks for American multinational firms that were "sending American jobs abroad". As a political issue, offshoring lost most of its power when George W. Bush won a second term, but as a populist economic issue and as a key cost reduction strategy on the part of companies in industrialized countries, it is an ongoing matter of concern. What drives offshoring – whether of manufacturing or of service provision – onward in the face of continuing attacks?

Economic activity moves from one country to another when productivity in the new location exceeds the costs of relocation, the liabilities of foreignness in the new location, and the barriers to reimporting the goods or services produced into the original market. China has become "the world's workshop" in the decades since Deng Xiaoping opened its markets to foreign firms and began the process of removing most state control of its economy in 1989. Many business firms entered China in the early years of the opening market seeking access to a market of over 1 billion potential consumers – who unfortunately had almost no money at the time. Even as the Chinese market failed to live up to hopes, though, manufacturing originally set up to service local markets shifted to production for export markets. The vast supply of underemployed labor combined with government subsidies intended to stimulate jobs growth and a currency fixed to the dollar to offer much lower manufacturing costs than anywhere else on the face of the earth . . . and consumers loved it. Wal-Mart, previously a bastion of "Made in America" quickly became China's largest trading partner. Textile plants that had left South Carolina for Mexico moved on to China. Taiwanese electronics companies found ways to avoid political barriers to set up clean room facilities on the mainland. Nike shifted sneaker production from other developing nations to China. And some economists warned that this accelerating process of "hollowing out" American corporations by offshoring production, whether to outsourcing specialists or through joint ventures, would eventually undermine the innovative capacity of these companies. However, corporations argued that they kept research, design, marketing, and other high value activities in their home markets, and the pricing advantages of low cost production in Chinese offshore facilities drove ever more companies, even those focusing strictly on domestic markets, to make their products in China – furniture, televisions, t-shirts, laptop computers, toys, and airliner subassemblies. And people adapted as lower prices relieved concerns for lost jobs. China's large population had a comparative advantage in manufacturing due to very low wages, and so long as high value jobs stayed in the US, the expanding American service economy could afford it.

The 2004 campaign revealed a new twist on this story – the rapidly increasing trend of offshoring business services – back office business processes, ICT services, help desks, and the like. While China is participating in this process, India – or at least several urban areas in India that offer strong local universities, large numbers of young and well-trained engineers and technicians with solid English language skills, and broadband connections to the world – is excelling at it. Software firms reached out to Indian companies during the Y2K reprogramming crisis, only to find that the inexpensive programmers and software engineers in India were capable of much more than simple line-by-line fixes to large programs. Over the next half-dozen years, increasingly sophisticated programming tasks were shifted to India, either through captive facilities or via outsourcing contracts, computer firms set up technical help desks, business service firms from the US and UK sent their database management tasks, and so forth. Suddenly, knowledge-intensive tasks requiring highly educated labor that were supposed to be the provenance of the industrial nations were following simple manufacturing to the emerging markets. The shocked reaction to this resulted in politicians and even economists questioning whether the presumed laws of comparative advantage had changed. However, what they failed to notice, but business had, was that the improving educational systems in India, China, Eastern Europe, and other emerging markets were turning out large (in absolute terms, even if small in proportion to local populations) numbers of skilled, intelligent, driven young workers that were much less expensive than very similar workers in the US and Western Europe. Since the technologies, programs, accounting systems, HR systems, and other tools that are needed to perform these services are highly mobile, particularly over the Internet or on the Worldwide Web, these workers can perform essentially identical tasks that can be easily integrated into the business systems of Western companies for dramatically lower labor costs than are available through Western workers. It turns out that comparative advantage is a dynamic concept, particularly advantage that is not tied to natural resources, weather, or masses of unskilled workers. This chapter addresses the role played by location-tied differences in a dynamic global system where ICT advances have made the real costs of transmitting knowledge and information negligible.

A question asked constantly of international strategists is "What is different about international strategy from business strategy in general?" As we have seen, many of the ideas, theories, models, and approaches taken from business strategy can be applied to strategy in the international context. It is the importance of context, of location, to international strategy that differentiates it from generic business strategy. A company such as Haier, the largest white goods manufacturer in China, demonstrates the importance of such considerations. The dominant competitor at home, and a major OEM supplier to companies in the industrial economies, Haier is trying to become an independent competitor in the US. However, they are discovering that without an established brand in the US, low prices alone are not enough to generate significant market share. Even the most prosaic bit of strategic maneuvering tends to require additional thought, greater effort, and more stringent execution to succeed on a worldwide basis. On the other hand, multinational firms can use their access to different locations, each with its own unique character, to develop the idiosyncratic, firm-specific resources and capabilities that are the basis for sustained competitive advantage. This chapter provides a summary of the various aspects of the contextual environment in which global strategies are planned and executed, and that force these strategies to be adapted constantly. Each of these issues is often the subject of an entire course or an entire book in and of itself, so they must be drastically shortened in this case. Our focus is on how these aspects of the global business environment (GBE) impact business strategies, rather than on a fully developed description of the phenomena themselves. As such, the offerings here are more introductory than comprehensive in nature, and, while providing essential information for the exercise of strategy, should be followed up by additional readings and education in each area subsequent to this course.

International Economics and Trade Theory

Business strategy is inherently concerned with economic issues, so this seems a good place to start the chapter. International trade has taken place for millennia, at least since the times of the Babylonian empire, from which written records of trade accounts survive.[1] For much of this time, trade really did take place between nations, as governments intervened in markets heavily, licensed traders, and taxed trade, and actual trading was done by individuals or small investment groups. The earliest model of trade has been described as mercantilism (though the term was created long after the activity). In this model, the goal of nations in trade was to export home produced goods in exchange for gold, silver, jewels, and other forms of easily convertible money equivalents, and to use this income to support armed forces to protect the nation and government. Private trading entities were expected to follow the dictates of the government of their home country – and to receive protection in exchange. While healthy for national governments and for favored merchants, this model of trade is less obviously beneficial to the citizens of trading nations. They are expected to produce for export trade, not for themselves, and typically receive relatively little for their efforts, as the government and large trading companies are likely to retain most profits. With trading licenses offering considerable potential value, they were typically restricted to a few large firms – resulting in the high levels of smuggling and piracy that characterized international trade prior to the late eighteenth century, which were the only ways for the common people or small organized groups to gain from the international movement of goods.

Wealth tended to accrue to the trading companies, such as the British or Dutch East India Companies, with their charters from their national governments, control of transport, and relatively large size. Manufacturers tended to be small, to have little influence, and to be unable to access other than very local markets on their own. Consumers had even less influence on the system. Governments preferred to export critically needed goods in exchange for currency or easily convertible forms of wealth, not for goods needed by their own populations. Of course, government could not really hope to eliminate imports, but taxes and tariffs were used to discourage local consumption of imported goods and to extract maximum payments from those not completely discouraged. Mercantilism was about trade to benefit governments, not the people that were "represented" by those governments, but in the heyday of this model of trade, monarchial governments were not overly concerned about the quality of life or the opinions of the great majority of their people. Nations sought colonies as sources of needed commodities that the parent country could not provide for itself, then forced colonists to accept terms of trade that were highly unfavorable to themselves in exchange for protection from foreign powers. This approach was likely to lead to rampant inflation at home when successful, as goods disappeared from local shelves and money was imported in greater quantities, and then to destabilize the very government that planned to profit most handsomely from these policies – not to mention revolutions in the colonies!

While mercantilism as the standard model of trade is typically associated with the pre-Industrial Revolution world, neo-mercantilist policies continue to appear in today's world. Much of the East Asian economic miracle, from Japan to South Korea to Taiwan to China, has been built on policies intended to encourage exports and discourage imports. At least in the modern world export earnings have increased incomes and built infrastructure, not just built armies and navies and provided luxuries to an aristocracy. Nevertheless, these policies have led to continuing trade disputes, demands that currencies be revalued, markets be opened, domestic consumption encouraged, and threats from trading partners to impose various trade barriers to better balance trade flows. Indeed, the ever more distorted movement of goods and investment of related income from China to the US is being assigned a degree of blame for the 2009 global economic collapse. Such policies on the part of the US and the European Union are also blamed in large part for the failure of the Doha Round of multinational trade negotiation – those countries want to export technology-heavy goods to the developing world while blocking, or at least controlling, imports of food and other commodity imports from that world. Even as economists proclaim the benefits of freer trade, political realities continue to drive "beggar thy neighbor" mercantilist policies in many sectors and countries.

Absolute advantage and The Wealth of Nations

Adam Smith brought an entirely new approach to international trade, as well as pin-making, in 1776 with publication of *The Wealth of Nations*.[2] Just as pin-making could be broken down into a series of steps and workers specialized to each step organized to pass the work in progress along, so countries could specialize in the production of certain goods to which they were most suited (by geography, weather, and other natural endowments) and trade with each other to the benefit of all. Smith saw the wealth of nations to be based not in the accumulated treasure of the national government, but in improved consumption possibilities for the people of each and of all countries. If each country specialized, then greater quantities of consumable goods could be generated from the same raw materials through increased efficiency, greater skills, better quality, and the like. If countries over-produced their favored products and traded, then the overall quantity of goods available around the world could be increased. As countries traded their surpluses, people everywhere would have a greater choice of superior and less expensive products to consume. So long as every country had an absolute advantage in the production of some desirable product, every country would gain from trade, encouraging further economic cooperation and incidentally discouraging military adventurism.

This concept seems fairly apparent in today's industrial world, and underlies policies of offshore production and globally dispersed value-adding chains. Not only can home consumer/voters be offered jobs and income (which neo-mercantilism promises), but they can be offered a wider array of less expensive products to consume. This seems to work – all we need to do is determine what we do best and redirect or compensate (or ignore – depending on the sensitivity of government to individual needs) workers and companies in previously domestic industries that are disadvantaged. Of course, we see regular denunciations of practices of 'sending jobs abroad', even as less expensive goods and greater wealth are celebrated. Of greater concern, though, are circumstances when nations find suddenly that activities that they seemed to dominate begin to move offshore. What happens if a country appears to have a disadvantage in every type of tradable good and service – a fear that was a rampant response to increasing offshoring of business processes and other services from the United States in the early 2000s?

David Ricardo and comparative advantage

The key insight that underpins neoclassical trade theory is attributed to David Ricardo, English economist and Member of Parliament.[3] This is the concept of comparative advantage, which proposes that even if a country has an absolute disadvantage to its trading partners in all traded goods (though formally developed in the case of two nations trading two goods, the model is generally considered to work with larger numbers), trade is still possible so long as the countries are not identically endowed with factors of production. Even if, say, Mexico has an absolute disadvantage compared to the US in producing both corn and television set assembly (more units of labor are required for each unit of output of both goods in Mexico), trade is still possible. If Mexican producers are relatively more efficient at producing one good, television sets for instance, in a ratio different than the US producers, it is still preferable for the US to concentrate on producing the good in which it is most efficient (corn), leaving Mexico to produce the TVs. Because Mexico would be wasting its resources in producing the second good rather than its preferred product, the two countries combined will produce more of both goods by specializing in their most efficiently produced outputs and trading to give consumers in both countries balanced consumption possibilities. Only if the US were so much larger than its trading partners that it could make up all of its domestic demand for both goods would trade be unneeded. Even in such a case, excess demand in Mexico for one or the other good would result in international prices high enough to shift US production toward exports, reducing the supply (and raising prices) of the good for which production was sacrificed – typically the less efficiently produced good, and encouraging imports from Mexico – at prices higher than if there was no production shifting, but lower than if there was no trade. So long as demand somewhere in the world is greater than can be satisfied by local supplies at an optimum price, and trade is permitted, relative or comparative advantage will drive two-way trade for even the most efficient producing countries.

How does this happen? In the example, better land for corn production, larger and more efficient farms, better use of machinery and fertilizers in production, and so forth make American labor highly efficient in producing corn. TV sets are produced in pretty much the same way in both countries (most such plants are actually owned by non North American firms, whether in the US or Mexico), so that the less expensive labor in Mexico is not much less efficient than the more expensive labor in the US. In the real world, we see that large-scale US Midwest factory farming has indeed driven many Mexican small farmers off the land – further increasing the supply of labor for manufacturing. And we see TV set manufacturing on a fairly large scale in *maquiladora* plants along the US border – though in plants with Korean or Japanese ownership.

As we see in the case of ICT offshoring, comparative advantage is not static, though often treated in such a fashion. In our opening example, we looked at the growth of offshore production of both goods and services to China and India. At one time not long ago, these two countries had great disadvantages in generating sophisticated goods and services. However, improving and growing educational systems in both countries have turned out large numbers of technically trained individuals faced with relatively little domestic demand. This has allowed these two countries, and others in Eastern Europe, though filled with poorly trained and educated labor, to develop large (in absolute terms) pools of skilled workers. Given the global availability of production processes, whether clean rooms for integrated circuits or programming techniques for software, these large pools of skilled but inexpensive workers have shifted comparative advantage from the United States to large emerging economies – and we will see that there are models for this evolution, even if Ricardo did not see it 200 years ago.

The factor availability model of comparative advantage

Ricardo's model of comparative advantage held sway for more than a century (at least among economists – as we have seen, governments seem to be caught up by mercantilist leanings even today), but certain anomalies led to further development of the comparative advantage idea in the early twentieth century. Ricardo considered the relative efficiencies of labor, based on local conditions or technologies, across countries for producing different goods. Eli Heckscher and Bertil Olin, working separately, moved beyond the focus on a single factor of production and also accounted for the fact that countries did not typically specialize completely in a single commodity.[4] By considering trade in two commodities, produced by the combination of two factors (labor and capital, typically), between two countries (later proven to hold for any number of countries, goods, and factors), and introducing the concept of declining economies of scale, the Heckscher-Olin model came a bit closer to observable reality. Where the Ricardo model implicitly assigned different "technologies" to different countries in order to explain different labor efficiencies, the H-O model assumed similar technologies would be available around the globe, and assigned efficiencies in production to the country with relatively more of a given factor. Thus, between two nations, the one with a relatively high labor to capital availability ratio would be expected to specialize in production of the labor-intensive good, while the other country would specialize in the capital-intensive good. Trade then allows consumption demand to be satisfied in both countries.

However, in each country specialized demand would tend to use up the more common factor faster than the less available factor until prices for that factor rose relative to the other and further specialized production became inefficient compared to the trading partner. Thus, each nation would produce more of the good that used its more common factor of production more intensively, but neither would completely specialize to eliminate all domestic production of the disadvantaged good. What *would* happen, as propounded by Samuelson, is that prices for factors (wages for labor, returns to capital) would be bid up in the country where they were initially lower due to excess supply, and drop in the country where they were initially higher as relative demand dropped even more with trade.[5] Thus we see that China, with its huge underemployed labor force, is already experiencing labor shortages and rising wages due to production for international markets, and the US, despite (or because of) a surfeit of capital, is experiencing downward pressure on wages for less skilled workers. The Indian example (now spreading to China as well) of shifting advantage in the provision of advanced services to companies and consumers in the US at first seems to fly in the face of the H-O model, because the largest part of the populations of these countries is still stuck with minimal skills for the modern world. However, as local demand has failed to provide employment for skilled workers, the underemployed pool of such labor in these countries is quite large – though hardly unlimited, as it turns out. Compared to the US, for instance, India has an oversupply of trained programmers and hence a factor availability advantage in this sector. Sectoral advantages are not necessarily identical to overall national resource endowments.

The International Product Life Cycle and shifting comparative advantage

One model that recognized the dynamism of comparative advantage and predicted large-scale shifts in production of even highly skilled jobs out of the industrial world was Ray Vernon's International Product Life Cycle.[6] Working in the 1960s, and observing the post-World War II world with a dominant US economy, Vernon suggested that innovations would arise in the US, where development and manufacturing would take place. As demand also developed in Europe, exports from the US would initially satisfy demand from that region. However, as production processes were standardized and host markets grew, production would shift out of the US (while higher value activities stayed) to Europe, and more standardized products would be imported to the US from there. At the same time, demand would begin to emerge in the less developed world. As the industry continues to mature, demand would slack in favor of new innovation in the US and eventually Europe, while increasing in LDCs. Cost pressures in these markets, and increasing price competition in the developed world would result in production shifting to labor-rich developing countries, and customers for a now-standard product in the US and Europe would be served by imports of goods that they previously exported.

Vernon's model, mentioned in the previous chapter, lost credibility when Europe and Japan emerged as economic equals of the US and life cycles of products in different regions collapsed into a single global product cycle. This formulation has become less relevant as the post-War world approached a more balanced distribution of economic activity. However, offshoring of manufacturing and business processes by companies in the US and EU shows that the essentially dynamic nature of comparative advantage that was recognized by Vernon is, if anything, increasing in a knowledge-driven world economy. We see that demand for business services in the emerging markets is developing much more slowly than overall demand for these services – Indian ICT services have expanded in response to international demand and under-used local supply that leads to highly productive output and comparative advantage. Where does such advantage, not based on natural endowments of resources, come from?

Constructed comparative advantage and Porter's diamond model

Traditional models of comparative advantage are based on "natural" – or at least externally established – endowments of factors of production: numbers of people, amount and fertility of land, amount of capital, mineral deposits, and so forth. These endowments are traditionally calculated at the national level and countries are expected to export preferentially products that are generated through relatively heavy use of a country's more common factors of production. However, as empirical estimates of comparative advantage have led to unexpected patterns, such as Leontieff's famously paradoxical discovery that the US in the 1960s apparently exported labor-intensive – not capital-intensive – goods,[7] and as competitive advantage of companies has come to be associated more with knowledge and technology, the focus on natural endowments of commodity factors has been recognized as inadequate. The modern focus has shifted to country characteristics associated with knowledge and innovation, characteristics largely created by human activity. These include educational levels, infrastructure, work ethic, levels of competition and incentives for innovation, demand characteristics, and the need to overcome limitations in natural endowments. The most familiar model that addresses "constructed comparative advantage" is Michael Porter's "diamond" of national competitive advantage.[8] Porter proposes that the interactions of four determinants – natural endowments (or shortages), sophistication of demand, industry sector competition, and strength of related and supporting industries and institutions – determine whether a country will have a "national competitive advantage" in an industry segment, demonstrated by the performance levels of companies in that industry based in that country. Porter finds that government policies toward education, infrastructure development, competition and collaboration, investment, and so forth are critical to providing a context in which industries can thrive.

Porter based his analysis on research conducted in the late 1980s, so many of his conclusions remain relevant, though shifts of manufacturing from Japan to Korea and Taiwan and now to mainland China, or the loss of advantage by many of the regionally concentrated "clusters" in Italy, show that this is a dynamic condition. This is hardly surprising, as man-made conditions are constantly changing. Success in an industry can breed complacency as much as further innovation, governments can interfere or cut funding, new discoveries can disrupt the entire technological pattern that has made one country strong in an industry. We also see that some parts of this pattern seem to be less fixed than originally proposed. For instance, local demand patterns are supposed to be critical to the development of industry sectors in a country. However, we see instances such as the development of the ICT sector in India in which local demand is apparently irrelevant. Rather, the needs of the developed world for a sudden massive increase in programming activity in response to the Y2K scare combined with the large population of trained programmers and computer science graduates coming out of India's technical universities to create a strong, even worldleading industry with little local demand or real competition – the market was big enough for all initially. In 2009, though, shrinking demand for business services on the part of struggling companies in the US and the EU is threatening continued growth in the technology sectors of these emerging market countries with few local customers.

Industry clusters – comparative advantage on the local level

At the same time that the idea of comparative advantage has shifted toward knowledge generation in innovative industries and away from natural endowments in commodity industries, the focus on relevant locations has narrowed from nations to localities. Porter applied his diamond to specific locations when he realized that Silicon Valley, not the US as a whole, had an advantage in semiconductors and computers; Sassuolo, not Italy, was superior in producing ceramic tiles; and Bangalore, not India, had an advantage in business process outsourcing.[9] Even in traditional commodity industries, factors such as farmland or mineral deposits are not distributed evenly across a country, and while some regions may excel in production of certain goods, others in the same country may have no production of these goods at all. Economic geographers have studied industrial clusters for decades, and international business strategy has picked up this idea in the last decade or two and used its analytical tools to begin to analyze why certain locations are superior for certain industries. One successful company and related spinoffs, suppliers, customers, and competitors can build a strong industry center in a particular location. You will recall the development of Luxottica from the first chapter. This company sprang from the "eyeglass cluster" in northern Italy, and had kept the majority of its design and manufacturing in that small area. Similarly, Benetton arose from a regional industry focused on knitwear, Acer from a cluster of computer component companies in Taipei, and the influence of Hewlett Packard and Fairchild Semiconductor on the early development of Silicon Valley is undeniable. Competition to sharpen innovation, supporting companies to collaborate in innovation, demanding local customers who reward innovation, and the physical, educational, financial, and cultural infrastructures to support innovation make such clusters highly effective.

Local firms become world beaters and multinational firms from other places set up local facilities to participate in the innovative atmosphere. As companies consider the role of location in enhancing competitive advantage, nations are becoming less relevant than local clusters to offering unique opportunities to succeed. As big emerging market economies like India and China begin to compete successfully in technology-intensive industries even while they

continue to offer the appearance of developing nations, many agree
with economists who have speculated that if India and China can
continue to out-compete the US in industries where "we have a
comparative advantage", then we are in trouble. Likely the case,
if true. However, the reality is that Bangalore and Shanghai have
comparative advantages in producing business services or computer
chips over competing locations in the US – and these comparative
advantages are often exploited for their own competitive advantage
by US, Japanese, and European firms. At the same time, the vast
hinterlands of China and India do *not* have comparative advantages
in technology-based industries. These countries as a whole excel in
low cost production of relatively low capability goods, as would
be expected. However, their large (in absolute numbers) but small
(as a proportion of population) educated populaces, concentrated in
a few metropolitan regions, act as "nations within nations" for the
purpose of economic analysis. They offer skill levels approaching
(in cases even surpassing) those of industrial economy workers at
much lower wages, even as the majority of the population struggles
to find adequate food and housing.

Comparative advantage and competitive advantage

The previous several sections have addressed different models of
how comparative advantage – that advantage tied to particular
locations – develops and is maintained (or lost). From an international economics perspective, this is an interesting issue in and of
itself, but from a global strategy perspective, the question must be
"How does this help my company to gain competitive advantage?"
Comparative advantage associated with a location is often the basis
of competitive advantage for companies based in, or invested in,
that location. Thus, ARAMCO gains an advantage in the oil business
by being tied to Saudi Arabian oil fields, where extraction costs are
the lowest in the world. Wipro gains an advantage in offering business process outsourcing because it is located in Bangalore, where
inexpensive, well trained Indian IT graduates are available. Intel
has built and maintained competitive advantage in semiconductors
thanks to its location in Silicon Valley, the worldwide center for
the industry (true partly *because* Intel is there), and is working to

maintain its competitive advantage by rapidly expanding its facilities in China and India by tapping into their lower cost, but adequately skilled, workforces. Companies have traditionally reflected the character of their home markets, and have benefited from their strong "diamonds", as is the case for Toyota and Honda in automobiles and the many other examples offered by Michael Porter.[10] Successful competition in tough home markets hones the competitive abilities of firms when they move to international markets and is the basis for the "Ownership Advantages" described by John Dunning in his Eclectic Model of Foreign Direct Investment. Firms based in a country or local area build on the commonalities of their location, even as the best of them add their own unique competencies to the skills demanded by the competition.

At the same time, multinational firms seek investment in locations with strong location-tied advantage in order to participate in that comparative advantage. Thus, many non American computer component firms have operations in Silicon Valley, just as many American firms have located operations in China, India, and other advantageous locations. For firms in industries from t-shirts to memory chips, production in China (actually Guangzhou, Shanghai, and several other cities and Special Economic Zones) is essential to maintaining competitive parity, much less comparative advantage, but for the most aware, new capabilities are being built in low cost production, character recognition, voice-based computing, and many other innovative areas of technology by virtue of locations in China and other emerging nations. Similarly, Japanese pharmaceutical companies in need of biotechnology-based innovation have invested in a wide range of development ventures with American biotech start-ups and university laboratories. Biotech research is stronger in the US than in Japan – but Japanese skills in the technologies needed for industrial scale production of biotech-based drugs are very high. Thus, the combination of location-specific competencies (in research) and company-specific competencies (in production – tied to traditional Japanese skills in fermentation technologies) are combined to provide world-class competitive advantage. As multinational companies seek competitive advantage in world and local markets, access to location-based comparative advantages from around the world can be used to build and leverage firm-specific advantages that can easily surpass local competitors.

Bruce Kogut describes how multinational firms can use comparative advantage to gain competitive advantage, and can add other benefits of differentiated location to become even more competitive.[11] He points out that as products move along their individual value-added chains, each activity has different economics – some are more labor-intensive, some require raw material inputs, some are highly automated, others require innovation and intellectual inputs. These various steps, if considered separately, can be matched to the comparative advantage aspects of different countries, so that by siting their operations optimally and then coordinating their supply chains carefully, multinational firms, and particularly highly integrated multinationals, can gain sustained advantage over firms that due to size, capabilities, or limited horizons, keep their value-adding activities in one country. Once activities are dispersed to efficient locations, the firm can then take advantage of multiple locations to pressure suppliers of factors of production (land, labor, capital, etc.) to keep prices low due to indirect competition with suppliers in other similar markets, they can arbitrage between markets to take advantage of lower prices, even in the short term, and they have advantages in bargaining with governments and regulatory bodies because they are not forced to operate at a disadvantage anywhere.

So we see that the basic economics of the international marketplace offer the possibilities of competitive advantage to multinational firms that can take advantage of differences across countries – however, exactly, those differences are defined. However, economic distinctions are hardly the only aspects of the international business environment that can impact the strategic choices of multinational firms. Political, legal and regulatory, and social and cultural differences between countries and regions limit MNCs as they consider where to make and sell products, but also give those companies that can get it right considerable advantage over their competition. In the next sections, I will cover some basic issues in each of these areas, and will add to this discussion when I look at entry strategies in Chapter 8. However, these are big topics – each is associated with one or more major fields of study in most universities, and their business implications are covered in depth in classes on the environment of international business, so I won't go into much depth on these topics here.

Country Risk Issues and the GBE

Political differences and international strategies

American politicians are fond of proclaiming the superiority of our representative democracy. Indeed, democracy of some sort has spread into countries around the globe, though this has hardly been without some difficulties for the United States and other industrialized countries. And, despite the increase in numbers of democracies, many economically important countries still have little or no political democracy.

Among democracies, the political perspective on business varies considerably. In general, political democracy is tied closely to a more or less free market – "economic democracy". However, just what this means to business can vary considerably. While allocation of goods and services is largely left to the forces of supply and demand, government may intervene, often through government-owned companies or through formalized support for the interests of labor – or capital. The "Anglo-American" view is typically taken to be that business and investment are generally positive influences, at least if adequately regulated. Capital investment is protected (lower capital gains tax rates in the US, for instance), shareholders are given protections, business is offered various benefits, and labor unions are permitted, but not given great encouragement. The Continental European perspective, albeit from an equally democratic system, is generally less friendly to private business. Many major companies have significant government participation and important subsidies, labor unions are given special privileges, and taxes remain relatively high on investment income. In Germany, for instance, workers are represented by national unions and labor is guaranteed positions on corporate supervisory boards. In France, the work week has been restricted to 35 hours, even for supervisory employees. And, as a senior executive in the European headquarters of a US multinational chemical company once told me with some surprise, "Labor is a fixed cost in Belgium!" That is, the cost of dismissing employees made adjusting the size of his workforce to match demand a financial impossibility.

Less democratic, even totalitarian, states host multinational firms as well. Some, such as the Peoples' Republic of China, have been generally welcoming to foreign investment and have become critical to multinational strategies – both as an offshore production platform and as a potentially huge market, in the case of China. Others are less welcoming – Venezuela and Russia both have strong presidents whose governments have recently been pressuring foreign energy multinationals to take on local partners for oil and gas development, or have actually forced the sale of assets to local government interests. A pro-business, centrally controlled, state can be very welcoming to business, as it can manage its political and economic interests very closely to minimize disruptions – or, at least it can crack down on dissidents effectively. On the other hand, changes in government direction can result in arbitrary judgments or sudden pressures against foreign companies – such governments and their policies often are not concerned with policy consistency, particularly when sudden opportunities to garner large hard currency windfalls.

Within and among these different systems, the biggest concerns for multinational strategy are the problems created by disputes between home and potential host governments and by changes in the local political scene in the foreign host country. In the former case, extremes such as open warfare or trade embargoes have obvious implications for businesses – certainly the Nazi government seized foreign-owned factories before World War II, and German companies saw their assets in the Allied nations likewise seized. Strong foreign support for a previous government can lead to selective loss of assets, often without immediate compensation, as happened to American interests in Cuba in 1959 and Iran when the Shah fell from power. These events are large and apparent, and can be quite harmful to a handful of companies. More economic threats come from smaller disputes, however. For instance, despite the generally strong political relationship between the US and the European Union, regular trade disputes linked to political disagreements have made certain goods from either side of the Atlantic more expensive, often prohibitively so, on the other side. Smaller companies trading in goods that suddenly become "symbolic issues", such as Italian pasta products or French red wines, can find their economic viability threatened by their own government – a minor sacrifice on the national level, but hard on the owners of small businesses.

Local political disputes or economic problems created as temporary sops to economic problems can likewise be very costly. Many developing countries use easy monetary policies to channel money to poor citizens in order to maintain jobs and reduce unrest, but resulting inflation and currency devaluation can hurt the hard currency profits of multinational firms, even when local business seems good. At other times, emerging economies have imposed limitations on exports of hard currencies, which can make obtaining inputs, paying investors, justifying capital investment, or even maintaining operations difficult. Local insurgencies can lead to violence against foreigners and employees of foreign companies as well as restricting consumers from markets. Enforced local partnerships with 'connected' individuals and organizations can drain funds and restrict strategic decisions. And, worse, poorly attuned foreign firms may not be really aware of such concerns until they have made their investments and put their resources and employees at risk.

Various agencies offer assessments of political risk, or the somewhat broader category of "country risk". Business Environment Risk Intelligence and similar services offer scoring systems looking at levels of risk, levels of freedom, or other quantifications of complex qualitative calculations. The Economist Intelligence Unit provides lengthy narrative assessments of many countries, as do the Central Intelligence Agency and other government and intergovernment agencies. Most international banks do risk assessments for their own investments and provide access to their customers. Even smaller banks and law firms maintain correspondent relationships with foreign counterparts and can offer country, industry, and even firm-specific advice that is timely and based on local knowledge, if perhaps limited in breadth. Companies, even smaller ones with little international experience, can access considerable information and informed opinion about political risks in other countries. The concern for multinational strategy is how to respond to possible threats, or even to established problems that might or might not impact any one company. Experience in international markets combined with internal risk assessment offices can help established, larger multinational firms, but even these companies and their well-thought-of advisors can be wrong at times. Strategic managers from smaller firms considering entering less stable, less friendly, less predictable national environments must recognize that good business opportunities can go bad quickly when the political situation changes.

Of course, many of the "big events" in world politics, from Castro's overthrow of the Batista government in Cuba, to the fall of the Shah in Iran, to the fall of the Soviet Union, to the Iraqi invasion of Kuwait in 1991, were unexpected, even shocking to the experts as much as to any casual observer. In addition, most losses to political and country risk are in the form of incremental reductions in cash flow to inflation, devaluation, punitive taxes, and the like, which are much less glamorous and noticeable than massive expropriations, but as important to address if we want profitable business activities in a wide array of nations.

Legal structures and property rights

Legal institutions vary considerably across nations. Three basic models dominate in today's world. British-influenced countries, such as the UK, US, Australia, Canada, and so forth take a common law approach, in which previous court decisions offer interpretations of legislation, and legal precedent is as important to decisions as written law. In much of the world, Napoleonic or civil codes depend strictly on the letter of laws passed by legislatures, and judges only apply laws, they do not interpret them. In the Islamic world, sharia law, or a legal structure based on the strictures of the Koran, is becoming more prevalent. Religious edicts and interpretations by religious scholars offer a variety of interpretations, but the sense that laws are a reflection of God's will make for stringent application of these codes in any location. These legal institutions are typically tied more to criminal than to commercial law, but the certainty of application of written laws can result in more or less environmental risk in various countries.

From a business strategy perspective, the major considerations involve commercial codes, property rights (particularly intellectual property rights in today's knowledge-focused world), civil law and consumer rights, tax laws, and the degree of enforcement of such codes. Companies engaged in foreign direct investment need to be familiar with requirements for local partnership, the availability and legitimacy of recourse in the case of contract disputes, and the variety of licenses and restrictions required to set up a business in any specific country. Companies doing business in the United States, well known for the commonality and size of civil suits against companies for a variety of injuries and complaints, from physical damage to monetary losses during stock market downturns, face real threats to their economic viability. In most other countries, even those with similar codes, the frequency and size of civil suits are much lower, and are often unenforceable. In the same way, most countries provide legal protection for property rights, but the level of enforcement and access to recourse varies greatly. Intellectual property protection varies more widely, as the levels of protection offered to patent, trademark, and copyright holders in industrial societies are often much higher than in developing countries, where the needs and demands of millions of poor consumers may outweigh the ability of foreign companies to extract profits from local markets. Thus, China has sufficient IP protection laws, but lax enforcement has led to estimates that as much as 90% of the software in the country is obtained illegally, imitation luxury goods are widely available, and Hollywood movies are available on bootleg DVDs before they are officially released in the US.

Legal and regulatory institutions restrict the activities of corporations, but also protect corporations in the legitimate pursuit of profits. High quality legal representation is essential in business, and is most important in foreign countries where the natural inclinations and home country-based assumptions of managers may be forbidden. So long as a well constructed and enforced legal structure is properly understood and followed, businesses may feel restricted but should not face major risks. However, irregular enforcement or a sense that enforcement is unlikely can lead companies to either ignore laws or to mistakenly engage in behavior that is subject to interpretation. While often offering high returns, such decisions can dramatically raise risks. For instance, in the early 1990s in Russia, complex, overlapping, and generally unforced tax laws led many local and foreign businesses to simply avoid reporting and paying taxes on income. While the overwhelmed legal system in Russia was unable to identify or prosecute many violators, a few large corporations faced severe penalties (or at least large legal bills), and many businesses found that they had no recourse in cases of contract violations because they were afraid to open their books to the authorities. More recently, a major liquefied natural gas pipeline on Sakhalin Island was closed down for unspecified "environmental violations" while Gazprom was engaged in an unfriendly attempt to take control of a joint venture with Shell and two Japanese minority partners. Once the European company accepted the inevitable and handed over the controlling interest to the local partner on punitive terms, the environmental issues apparently evaporated. The risks of working in a poorly developed, unevenly enforced, and hence unpredictable legal system can offer opportunity to the highly entrepreneurial, but are threatening to established companies that are more interested in protecting their interests and maintaining their reputations.

Cultural heritage and business

Besides the great variations in political and legal institutions around the world, sociocultural institutions may offer the greatest challenges to multinational corporations. While less likely to result in seizure of assets or imprisonment of managers than violations of the more formal national institutions, failures to understand and incorporate cultural demands can result in ongoing loss of competitive advantage and eventual business failure in foreign markets, often with no sense by managers that the company has done anything wrong. Sociocultural differences hit companies in three main places. First, and perhaps most important, consumers in any national or subnational market may find goods and services to be lacking in key dimensions. Even what seems to be a relatively small violation of local norms can vastly limit market potential, and unexpectedly offensive products can do real damage to a company's prospects in a country for years to come. Product names, colors, slogans, packaging, and the like have all been pointed out as accidentally offensive, humorous, foolish, or otherwise unsuited to selling product effectively.

Second, the operations of a company in a foreign culture can violate local norms, so even though its products are acceptable, its means of production, distribution, defense of intellectual property, or a variety of other activities may be seen as offensive. Many strong cultural demands are incorporated in local legal structures, which can put companies in real legal jeopardy, but others may be equally as strong while not supported by law – or even in contradiction to local laws. Thus, cultures of bribery in many developing nations are seldom protected under local law – bribery of local officials is almost always illegal – but many companies find that operating in compliance with the law but in violation of custom is costly and difficult. Knowing how, when, how much, and to whom gifts are customarily given (and when a gift becomes a payoff) is critical to gaining goodwill in many cultures, and can be a great challenge to companies from countries such as the US, where gift-giving in commercial transactions is less common. Many scholars suggest that intellectual property losses in China, and the difficulty of ending these through legislation, owe much to traditional Chinese attitudes toward knowledge that generally consider knowledge to be public property that *should* be shared freely among interested parties.

Third, cultural differences can have major implications for hiring, retaining, and inspiring local employees. American companies tend to expect employees to sacrifice much of their private lives to perform their jobs, even when problematic. However, in collective cultures with strong family or group identities, the idea of going to work with a sick child at home, or putting the needs of the office ahead of the needs of a relative, may be seen as abhorrent. In cultures with strong national identities, such as Japan or Korea, simply working for a foreign company can be seen as a subtle (or not so subtle) betrayal of cultural expectations, and can make hiring highly qualified workers difficult for MNCs. It has taken years for multinationals in Japan and Korea to raise the interest of the best graduates of the best schools in taking employment with them.

Stories of cultural misunderstandings are myriad, but do seem to come down to losing customers, violating norms of organizational behavior, or offending (even driving away) workers. Multinational firms that have considerable international experience, and particularly those that have tried to cultivate a multiethnic or global mindset, can avoid many of these problems. Ethnocentrism can be a great detriment to doing business internationally, but can be avoided through a bit of common sense and the recognition that cultures do vary and that assertions of cultural superiority are bad for business (even in cases where managers may feel them!). Your customer may worship a different god, eat foods that you find unpalatable, treat dogs and children in ways that seem medieval, and take different holidays, but he or she is still your customer. If you don't respect his or her needs, you still won't make a sale. Most multinational companies are well beyond such "ugly American" or "colonial master" or "righteously indignant" phases, although really taking a global perspective of local cultural acceptance while still maintaining the basic corporate cultural identity (often rooted in home cultural assumptions) is much more challenging.

Emerging markets and the bottom of the pyramid

New issues arise regularly in the international business environment. At the beginning of the twenty-first century, the great change is the emergence into the consuming world of several countries with very large populations, but relatively small (if large in absolute terms) modern segments of their economies and societies, and with remaining populations ranging from underemployed to impoverished and from large to truly huge. These include both countries emerging from totalitarian socialism as part of the Soviet bloc, to include Eastern Europe and Russia, and countries emerging from simple poverty and economic isolation, such as India and Brazil, and those that were mired in both conditions, such as China and Vietnam. This phenomenon has opened a new model for international strategies. Strategists have long recognized that less developed or developing markets are different from the industrialized world in resources, demand, capabilities, and potential. What has become more important, as these countries become more open markets, is that the size of their populations, combined with economic opportunity, makes possible tremendous growth, sustainable over a long period.

Eastern Europe, with a population that has added some 50% to the European Union, even with some countries still outside the EU, also has relatively well educated, relatively sophisticated workforces, but with underemployment holding down wages. As Poland, Czech Republic, Hungary, and the rest of Eastern Europe become the workshops of Europe they are also rapidly becoming a major new market for goods produced throughout the region. Any medium to large size European company must consider both producing and selling in the East. Russia appeared to be in much the same situation, but with its growing oil and gas wealth is trying to re-establish itself as a world power. It is an essential, if volatile, player in energy and resources markets, and is becoming more of a consumer of goods from the West as well. However, rising political tensions appear to have slowed the rush to do business in this vast country – and have made some existing investments appear rather questionable.

India and Brazil are the largest countries in their respective regions. Neither country was part of the Communist sphere in the late twentieth century, but both pursued import replacement investment strategies, seeking independence from the perceived economic imperialism of the West. As a result, both countries languished for decades with vast potential but little performance, and with very large populations of the unemployed or underemployed. Both countries have made dramatic and sustained moves into the international economy over the last 10 to 15 years, though. Their relatively small modern industrial sectors are becoming important competitors in certain world markets – Embraer is a major supplier of commuter airliners and Brazil is the leading country in generating alcohol-based fuels, while from India various Tata companies, Mittal Steel, and assorted IT providers are major forces in world markets. At the same time, the large populations of these countries are seeing new income, with the result that they represent some of the fastest growing markets in the world. Large (in absolute terms, if not in relative size) emerging middle classes are looking for automobiles, computers, entertainment, and the other accoutrements of modern life. At the same time, authors such as C.K. Prahalad proclaim that even the poorest among these populations have sufficient wealth, as a group, to offer opportunities to multinational companies that can solve the riddle of microdistribution. Prahalad proposes that by bringing needed goods to the bottom of the economic pyramid, companies can make fortunes while also offering many individuals the chance to begin to raise their own living standards.[12] The idea of economic development through capitalism at levels of poverty long seen as below the horizon for international business – even if more difficult and riskier than presented – seems to have caught on as a new possibility for growth in an ever more saturated world market.

Of course, no look at the emergence of market economies would be complete without addressing the rise of China and other Asian ex-Communist states such as Vietnam. Rather than going through the political upheavals of Eastern Europe and Russia, these countries have maintained centrally controlled, even totalitarian, states with the local Communist Parties dominating the political scene. However, these parties and governments have largely divested themselves of responsibility for controlling their economies from the center. The resulting economic booms combined with relative political stability have been very attractive to multinational firms. China has rapidly become the workshop of the world, underpricing even the poorest of European or Latin American countries. At the same time, the massive inflows of foreign exchange have generated a booming consumer economy, and those billion or more Chinese have actually become a large and growing market for everything from natural resources to consumer goods at last. No major Japanese or American, and increasingly, European, firm can afford not to be in China, both to produce goods (and increasingly, services) and to sell their products. This same pattern seems to be repeating itself in other emerging Asian countries, whether they are emerging from central planning or simple economic chaos. And, as the demand for labor has driven up its price in China, companies are beginning to look to even "less emerged" economies such as Vietnam, or even coastal Africa.

The "Big Thing" in the international business environment today, then, is the emergence of nations with perhaps a total three billion people from economic isolation driven by political and nationalistic policies. Multinational firms must take, and are taking, note of the phenomenon. Production is shifting to these countries in a rejuvenated international product life cycle, but so is consumption – if at a slightly slower rate. Even as the political and economic systems of the industrial world are reacting with fear and nationalistic fervor to job outflows, they are embracing less expensive goods and services and feeling the effects (both good and bad) of these vast new markets. China is buying airplanes from Boeing and Airbus even as it puts textile producers around the world out of business and forces up oil prices to fuel its millions of new automobiles. Fortunes will be lost as well as made, but the emergence of perhaps two-thirds of the human population into the world market cannot be ignored. For multinational strategists, this sort of sea change in the IBE makes the usual considerations of industry and competitive analysis seem relatively trivial. This is where international strategy becomes so much more challenging than business strategy without a context.

SUMMARY

Environmental effects can come from a variety of sources, some of which have been discussed in this chapter – basic economic considerations, political differences, legal considerations, and sociocultural environments. Some key concerns in each area are detailed, but there are many more issues in each area of the IBE than can be even mentioned here. The dimensions or aspects that have been assigned to culture alone are myriad, as every anthropologist and sociologist has ideas on the subject, and even the major scholars are too numerous and differentiated to discuss in detail in a strategy text. For anyone actually engaged in the practice of international business, economists, international lawyers, and cultural trainers are easily located. Various agencies, from the CIA or the Economist Intelligence Unit to your local bank, can offer detailed analyses of country risk for most countries. Other sources offer scores for political risk, economic development, legal institutions, and the like for all countries. The key takeaway from this chapter is that multinational strategies must give explicit consideration to differences across national environments and to the international environment created by the interactions of nation states as well as to the industry and competitive environments that are the usual focus of business strategy, and which are covered in the next chapter.

Key Points in the Chapter

1 The Global Business Environment provides the context for global strategy.
2 International economics is dominated by the idea of comparative advantage – that different endowments and activities in different countries make them relatively more or less efficient at different economic activities. Specialization in those value-adding activities in which a country is favored and free international trade make for the most efficient distribution of activities worldwide.
3 Where earlier models of comparative advantage focused on natural endowments of resources, more recent approaches focus on advantages built through human endeavor.

4 Differences in political and legal systems can create vast misunderstanding, risk, difficulty, and tremendous opportunity in seeking arbitrage opportunities.

5 National cultural heritages likewise influence attitudes toward business, economics, risk, and responsibilities among many other concerns and have had profound effects on products and companies that attempt to engage in these markets.

Notes

1 Moore, K. and Lewis, D. (1999) *Birth of the Multinational: 2000 Years of Ancient Business History – From Ashur to Augustus.* Copenhagen: Copenhagen Business School Press.

2 Smith, A. (1869) *An Inquiry into the Nature and Causes of the Wealth of Nations, Book IV.* Oxford: Clarendon Press. First published in 1776.

3 Ricardo, D. (1967) *The Principles of Political Economy and Taxation.* Homewood, IL: Irwin. First published in 1817.

4 Ohlin, B. (1933) *Interregional and International Trade.* Cambridge, MA: Harvard University Press.

5 Samuelson, P. (2004) "Where Ricardo and Mill rebut and confirm arguments of mainstream economists supporting globalization", *Journal of Economic Perspectives*, 18: 135–146.

6 Vernon, R. (1966) "International investments and international trade in the product life cycle", *Quarterly Journal of Economics*, May: 190–207.

7 Leontief, W. (1953) "Domestic production and foreign trade: the American capital position re-examined", *Proceedings of the American Philosophical Society*, 97: 331–349.

8 Porter, M.E. (1990) *The Competitive Advantage of Nations.* New York: The Free Press.

9 Porter, M.E. (1998) "Clusters and the new economics of competition", *Harvard Business Review*, November–December: 77–90.

10 Porter 1990, n. 8 above.

11 Kogut, B. (1985) "Designing global strategies: comparative and competitive value-added chains", *Sloan Management Review*, Summer: 15–28.

12 Prahalad, C.K. (2005) *The Fortune at the Bottom of the Pyramid: Eradicating Poverty through Profits.* Philadelphia: Wharton School Publishing.

CHAPTER 4
Global Competitive Analysis

Strategy in Action

In the early 1970s, the American automobile industry had settled into a comfortable pattern. General Motors had a greater than 50% share of the North American auto market, with Ford in a distant second place and Chrysler falling in place as the last of the Big Three. Sure, American Motors still sold a few cars and a few more Jeeps, and college professors and their ilk drove BMWs, Volvos, or other European sedans with good handling, lower power, and better gas mileage. A few real nonconformists even drove strange looking, underpowered, Japanese coupes and sedans. Comfortable in their size, the Big Three saw no threats on their industry horizon, and took their styling, performance, and quality cues from each other. Unfortunately, as it turned out, their persistent focus on the big American domestic market led them to ignore the larger global industry.

When gasoline prices shot up in response to the Arab boycott after the 1973 Yom Kippur war between Israel and various Arab countries and again in 1979 at the instigation of the Shah of Iran, American car companies were caught off-guard with few small, efficient models. The Japanese, honed to a keen competitive edge in their very competitive (eight firms in a smaller market than the US with its three firms) home market, rapidly increased exports to the US but were still not able to keep up with the demand for smaller, fuel efficient cars. Despite subsequent pressure by the US government on the Japanese government to set up export quotas, followed by the Japanese manufacturers building plants and starting production in the US, this initial toehold was able to support the expansion of Toyota, Honda, and Nissan over the next 30 years as General Motors gave up half of its market share, Chrysler was acquired (and then spun off in failure) by DaimlerBenz, and Ford struggled to be profitable. The Big Three faced many difficulties, but ignoring the global aspect of their industry left them wide open to the Japanese challenge, as we shall see in this chapter.

The American companies could have responded to shifts in the market by developing successful smaller vehicles – they had the skills in their European subsidiaries. However, they thought that the customer focus on fuel efficiency would change soon enough (and they were right about that in the 1980s), and put their focus on a political strategy to limit Japanese imports. With the support of the United Auto Workers union, this resulted in the mantra that "if only the Japanese faced our costs, we could compete", and governmental threats of tariffs or quotas. Then the Japanese manufacturers did what economists expected and undertook a steadily growing program of foreign direct investment in the US, and post-NAFTA in Canada and Mexico. Avoiding unionization by building in right-to-work areas, their newer plants used more efficient processes to turn out the same well-designed cars with the same quality standards as Japan continued to cut into Big Three sales and profits. Over time, production of less expensive models has largely shifted to North America, while the trade quotas were used to import new luxury models. Japanese auto suppliers were pressed to set up local production, and American workers trained in Japanese production methods. And for the next 30 years, first Chrysler, then Ford, and now even General Motors have been surpassed by Toyota in total US sales, losing both share and profits in a struggle to control the industry without investing more than necessary in products or production plants. Now, of course, Chrysler and GM have gone bankrupt, with Chrysler to be an arm of Fiat, and GM likely to emerge stripped of most of its international assets and several core brands.

Not only is competition within a global industry often stronger, yet harder to evaluate than for domestic-only situations, but the macro-environment often complicates issues of industry analysis that would be relatively simple in the firm's home market. So, for instance, companies from all of the major industrial countries have been working to penetrate the mainland China market since Deng Xiaoping opened

China to competition in 1979. Many of these firms, convinced that "a billion Chinese who don't have any [fill in the blank with whatever we make]" would desperately want to spend their money on Western goods soon found otherwise. However, American companies, particularly General Motors, have had some success in China. Buicks became the favored ride of bureaucrats and the company was able to tie in with top local partners. Small cars from South Korean affiliates found a rapidly growing customer base as more Chinese workers entered the export economy. The economic crash of 2008–09 has hit GM hard in China as well as the US, though. With exports dropping and workers losing jobs, the boom in car sales has gone flat. GM's aging models, and doubts about the solvency of GM, have cut into sales at the same time that European models from Mercedes and BMW are growing in popularity among the wealthy and connected, while local companies and mass market Japanese and European models have advantages over Korean designed and built General Motors models. Even as American companies are looking to China for growth, more nimble competitors that are more in tune with local customers seem to be taking over the market. Sound familiar? Yet, fully aware of where future growth will occur, GM hopes to retain its position in China even as it sells off its European assets.

Industry Analysis and the Global Marketplace

Industry and competitive analysis as performed in business strategy can certainly be applied to international and global industries. However, when doing so, two considerations must be taken into consideration. First, in relation to global markets, it is essential that the global scope of such industries be matched by global horizons in the analysis. Second, when entering new local markets, firms should conduct local competitive analysis – while keeping in mind that any local market may be influenced by competition in the international market. One perspective on business strategy, based in industrial organization economics and popularized by the Harvard Business School and Michael Porter in particular, ascribes competitive success to industry characteristics and the firm's placement in its industry. Not all strategy scholars believe that industry determines performance, as we shall see, but the character of competition in the industry does interact with the capabilities of each and every firm to help determine its level of performance. The most commonly applied framework for industry analysis is the Five Forces Model developed by Porter.[1] This model proposes that five forces interact to determine the level of competition in any industry (or industry segment, for that matter). This model is equally relevant in a regionalized or globalized industry or segment, but must be seen on a global scale. Other models of industry analysis are often used by international strategists, most of which are compatible with the Five Forces Model (indeed, one was developed by Porter himself). Let's look first at the Five Forces Model in a global setting, and then at some of these complementary models.

The Five Forces Model in the global setting

The Five Forces Model was proposed in *Competitive Strategy* by Michael Porter. It is set in the ideas of industrial organization (IO) economics, which in general ascribed firm performance to membership in a high-performing industry.[2] IO economics maintains that performance is eroded for an industry as competitive conditions approach perfect competition, and that performance is protected by limiting entry so that oligopolistic competition conditions can be maintained. Incumbent firms try to establish and maintain barriers to new entry and to identify and occupy favored market positions that allow them to dominate the competition and increase market share and market power to extract near-monopoly prices. When industry structure is favorable, incumbent firms can stay profitable for extended periods, but if one or more of the forces is unfavorable, long-term profitability will suffer.

The forces are (see Figure 4.1):

1 Threat of New Entry – the possibility that as more firms enter the industry, increasingly competitive markets will reduce profit potential.
2 Threat of Substitutes – the possibility that new products or technologies will make the existing firms obsolete.
3 Bargaining Power of Suppliers – the possibility that one (or a few) specialized supplier(s) will have increased bargaining power and will extract the excess profits from the industry.

Porter's Industry Analysis

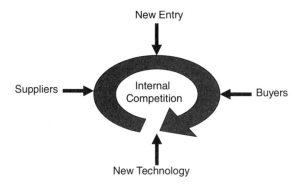

Figure 4.1   The industry Five Forces Model (after Porter, M.E., 1980).

4 Bargaining Power of Buyers – the possibility that a limited set of customers in comparison to the number of rivals will have the bargaining power to extract excess profits for *themselves*.
5 Rivalry among Incumbents – the possibility that direct competitors will be unable to coordinate actions and will compete away profits among themselves.

Given the microeconomic focus of this model, the key to the model is the threat of new entry. If the industry is profitable, microeconomic models say that more firms will enter until only normal returns remain. Porter suggests a variety of issues that will limit new entry and act as barriers to entry: brand loyalty, economies of scale and price competition, proprietary or otherwise closed distribution channels, high development costs for new products, or high capital investment demands are among them. Incumbent firms have these assets, outsiders do not, and the investment needed to acquire them is so high that potential entrants, typically much smaller firms, cannot expect to survive to profitability. The opening of global markets has created considerable turmoil by throwing out some of these assumptions. As in the case of Japanese auto makers, large foreign producers can enter a national market with the size and assets to go head-to-head with the incumbents of the domestic industry. Of course, American manufacturers found this to be the case when they spread into Europe and Latin America in the post-war era, but they were greatly surprised when Japanese companies were able to "come out of nowhere" only a few decades later in automobiles, consumer electronics, computers, robotics, and a variety of other manufacturing industries. If a firm plans to protect itself with barriers to competition, it must know who the competition is – all of it – and what it can do, or the complacency that seems inevitable among large firms in not very competitive industry sectors will lead to sudden downfalls.

Closely tied to the threat of new entry is the threat of substitute products, services, or technologies, because these can open the door to new and even replacement entry. In the example of the Japanese automobile industry and the US market, we see that small, fuel efficient, well made Japanese cars became suddenly attractive to Americans in the wake of two fuel crises in the 1970s that led to dramatically higher gasoline prices. American manufacturers had largely ignored the small car segment as unprofitable with low demand, and indeed Japanese imports had languished for many years. However, a changing world made small cars viable substitutes for many Americans, opening the way for Toyota, Nissan, Honda, and others. In addition to a different product focus, the Japanese firms had honed their production processes to drive their costs down as far as possible in their home market, so they could make a profit in a price segment that had long eluded General Motors and Ford. Japanese entry to the US market in other industries was tied to innovative products (often smaller but more reliable and more productive), new market approaches (store brands, direct sales rather than leasing, OEM supply to known brands), and superior technologies (computer controlled industrial equipment, robotics, solid-state circuitry) all applied before American firms (often the innovators, but not willing to make the investment in new plant and equipment to bring the technology to the marketplace on a large scale) could respond effectively. Again, internationalizing markets can change the terms of competition in ways unanticipated by firms accustomed to primarily local competition.

The buyer-supplier relationship is likewise affected by international markets. As most firms are both customers and suppliers along the value chain, their relative power may vary greatly depending on just what processes are under discussion. However, the currently hot issue of offshore manufacturing in East Asia reflects this issue. The only way many manufacturing firms can remain competitive is to use Chinese, Vietnamese, or other Asian suppliers. American and Western European suppliers cannot compete on price, and their large customers simply switch production to captive plants or contract manufacturers with a price advantage. This works very well for multinational firms in the industrial countries today; but as Chinese suppliers grow, combine, and drive out American competitors, the future looks precarious for the profits of large name-brand firms that have become committed to Chinese inputs. The essence of bargaining to appropriate more of the profits in a value-added chain is small numbers – the side with more competitors is more likely to accept less as the number of alternatives rises. Opening up to world markets raises numbers on all sides, but can drastically change relative bargaining power in countries that have been through industry consolidations.

Nor is there an easy fix for this problem. When US-based semiconductor chip suppliers complained of dumping on the part of Japanese memory chip suppliers in the 1980s, the federal government used trade actions and threats to drive up Japanese prices. As a result, American chipmakers had a short period of relief, but prices of US made computers were forced upward as well, opening the US market to Japanese personal computers – which had a much higher value and were made by the same consumer electronic companies in Japan. The artificially high prices of chips in the US then induced Korean manufacturers to take advantage of their much lower production costs to drastically increase output and flood the American market. In the end, US chipmakers largely went out of the memory chip business, US computer makers faced new price competition and rapidly lost share, and the Korean economic miracle found yet another market. Government intervention is often involved in attempts to manipulate supply chains and prices across national boundaries, and unintended consequences abound.

The same might be said of rivalries in global markets. Porter says that internal competition is tied to market positioning of firms as cost leaders, product differentiators, or niche players.[3] Tools such as market segmentation, in order to understand exactly who are our customers and who are our rivals for those customers, or measures such as concentration ratios, which can tell us how intense is the competition among those rivals, are critical to this analysis. In a stable, well defended industry, incumbent firms tend to settle into habitual patterns that maximize profits, often to the detriment of competition. Opening up to international markets leads to new ways of pursuing any of these strategies, but it also introduces an entirely new set of competitors, many of whom may have very similar ideas of what position to take within the market structure, and tends to increase competition and add considerably to the complexity of industry structure. Just as opening the US to Japanese rivals in many industries has had profound effects on the American economy (not to mention the Japanese economy), reducing trade and investment barriers to American firms forced European industries of all types to deal with much tougher competitive conditions.

We see the effects of globalized competition in many industries. International acquisitions and alliances have begun to reduce the number of independent automakers, as the Americans buy up or buy into European, Japanese, and Chinese producers, European firms buy (DaimlerChrysler – with a spinoff of the remaining husk of Chrysler to private equity investors) or ally with (Renault – Nissan) foreign competitors, and Chinese producers look for foreign partners and foreign targets. Boeing is allowed to buy McDonnell-Douglas because Airbus continues to provide tough competition from Europe. Firms look to foreign low cost suppliers to become or remain low cost producers in many industries. And governments are asked to provide protection from competitive forces around the world. Latin America is in the process, at least in a few countries such as Venezuela and Bolivia, of attempting another round of economic isolationism. The EU maintains the Common Agricultural Policy in the face of high food prices and increasingly strident demands from the developing world. American companies compete through anti-dumping lawsuits, political contributions, and blaming unions for high costs. Competitive turmoil is common in many industries, protectionism is contemplated more and more, industry consolidation with a worldwide scope is ongoing, all because rivalry in many industries has shifted from national to regional to global arenas in a very few years. Industry structure is a much more complicated issue internationally, and the impact of outside forces from the political, cultural, and legal environments on competitive conditions is much more noticeable than in domestic industry.

In addition to considering the five forces of industry competition from a global perspective, firms that are entering new foreign markets should consider the possible character of industry competition within those markets. Even as the American Big Three auto makers needed to look at the global industry to understand their real competition, so the Japanese car makers looking at the US market needed to understand the character of that market in order to attack it effectively. Likewise, as the global automotive industry closes in on the Chinese market, companies need to understand both the global and the local aspects of their competition. Each of the multinational competitors, much like GM, is trying to determine how their models stack up against their worldwide competition, when they might consider partnering, and how China can fit into their global plans. At the same time, Chinese auto firms are rapidly learning how to compete directly against the multinationals as well as cooperating with them. Many of these firms are connected to governmental bodies, have ties to foreign partners (some of which seem currently to be under consideration for revision), have copied essential aspects of foreign demand, and so forth. Further, Chinese consumers have fairly well developed ideas (whether accurate or not) about the characteristics of foreign firms from different countries, preferring local brands at the value end of the spectrum and American (now European) at the more expensive end. As GM and its global competitors look to China as the next major competitive market, they need to understand the quirks of that market as well as the actions and reactions of their multinational competitors.

International and global industries

Strategies of internationalization and globalization are driven by industry conditions, as in Porter's industry-driven model of configuration and coordination,[4] and are the consolidated outcome of multiple firm-level decisions in an environment consisting of other firms, suppliers, and customers, not a pre-existing competitive landscape. As in the case of the Five Forces Model, though, even if we attribute ultimate strategic success to firm-specific resources and capabilities and good strategic decision-making, the overall competitive conditions of an industry will influence multinational strategic decisions and will certainly have a part to play in determining how successful individual firm strategies are.

Just as firms may be more or less international in focus, so industries and segments may be more or less widely spread across nations. From a strategic perspective, this is not simply an issue of how similar markets may be across nations (though that is part of the issue), but also raises the question of international spread for all of the firm's activities. That is, while we are selling products around the world, are we also supporting R&D, manufacturing, sourcing, and other upstream activities in multiple countries? Some industries seem to reward a widespread presence, others a narrower set of horizons, yet others may suggest consistency across markets in only a portion of their value-adding activities, as national capacities vary greatly. The value of global integration also varies across industries. In some, economies of scale, similarities of demand, and technological consistency reward firms that can approach the world as one; but in other industries, local idiosyncrasies of demand and limits to available factors of production may force firms to adapt dramatically from market to market, both in marketing and in manufacturing.

Global integration and national responsiveness   Most industries offer some benefits to international scope, but they vary considerably on the rewards to global integration, which requires similar operations and products around the world, central control, and maximum efficiencies from scale economies. Other industries, however, benefit firms that can offer distinctive products in different national markets, products tailored to local needs and preferences. C.K. Prahalad and Yves Doz (and a variety of subsequent authors) considered Global Integration and National Responsiveness to be independent dimensions of strategy driven by industry characteristics.[5] Industries characterized by price competition, extreme concentration, high capital investment, a technological focus, and that are subject to economies of scale in the production of standardized goods or services are particularly likely to reward global integration. Integration treats the world (or at least a major region of it) as a single market, with customers everywhere interested in a standard product, either because a mature industry has settled on a dominant design and price competition, or because customers everywhere are interested in modern technologies that vary little from place to place. Firms move toward large size and large investments, whether in limited numbers of world-scale production facilities or in large, world-class research and development facilities – or both. At the same time, coordinating operations based in the most efficient and effective locations to squeeze the most from comparative advantage enables these companies to gain further cost advantage. Any industry in which the minimum efficient scale of production is greater than what can be absorbed by a single national market is likely to move toward becoming a single global market.

Not all industries are characterized by scale economies, technology, and/or price competition, though. Consumers of many products have fairly specific demands that vary widely from place to place. National customs, religious limitations, national security, and other similar considerations make national or sub-national markets unique. Economies of scale are small enough that much larger scale production offers only small cost benefits, such that slightly lower prices do not tempt most customers to alter their demand patterns, and companies must produce unique goods and services for local markets. In this case, international spread means adaptation to many local markets, with a focus on differentiating products for each geographical customer group, and possibly for different demand characteristics even within national markets. Companies that are less responsive to unique demand characteristics will lose customers to those that can exactly match demand in each market. Cost leadership typically offers too slight a price difference to make up for unsatisfactory product characteristics, unlike in global industries where slight differences in demand preference can be overcome by larger price differences. In this case, strategies that focus on responsiveness to national or local demands – geographically oriented differentiation strategies – are most likely to succeed. In practice, multinational firms in such an industry are likely to organize largely autonomous subsidiaries in different national and regional markets and to compete largely as local firms, albeit backed up by the financial, technological, and brand power of a much larger firm.

A key addition to the integration–responsiveness model of global strategy came from Chris Bartlett of Harvard Business School (HBS) and Sumantra Ghoshal, then at INSEAD after graduating from HBS.[6] They added a third dimension, international learning, to the integration and responsiveness dimensions. While a seemingly minor adaptation, the resulting Transnational Firm became the idealized form for multinational companies for a decade. The learning dimension suggested that a third way for multinationals to succeed was to generate superior innovation and spread it quickly and effectively throughout the globally dispersed company. This introduced the idea that a company could integrate across national boundaries, not to cut costs, but to offer a product differentiated on the basis of innovative technology, branding, design, quality, or other world-beating assets rather than adaptation on a market by market basis or simple cost minimization.

Configuration and coordination Michael Porter offers a model of international industry that builds on his Five Forces Model of industry analysis and reflects many of the same considerations as the Global Integration–National Responsiveness model.[7] Contrast Porter's model with the simpler one above. Porter recognizes explicitly that concentration of activities and geographical spread are not necessarily opposing considerations. He suggests that industries can be characterized by two dimensions: Configuration, which runs from concentrated to dispersed, and Coordination, which runs from low to high. Porter describes four corner conditions, as shown in Figure 4.2. High concentration and low coordination National Strategies emphasize home-based economies of scale, with most production in and for the home location and international markets served largely by casual exports – requiring little internal coordination across markets. Dispersed configuration and low coordination characterizes an industry that favors nationally responsive strategies, with activities widely spread and operated independently – most local markets served by local production in what Porter refers to as a multi-domestic strategy. High concentration and high coordination reflect what Porter calls a simple global strategy, in which

**Porter's International Terms of Competition
and Related Generic Strategies**

Global Coordination (Integration)

		Low	High
	Dispersed	Multi-Domestic	Complex Global Integration
International Configuration (Internationalization)			
	Concentrated	International	Simple Global (Scale Focus)

Figure 4.2 Configuration–Coordination (after Porter, M.E., 1986).

activities are concentrated, often in the home market and other major markets – thus combining comparative advantages of location with scale economies, and being coordinated across markets – very much the globally integrated strategy of Doz and Prahalad. Finally, Porter looks to dispersed configuration with high coordination as the globally integrated strategy that can balance demands for efficiency to compete in the industry with demands from location for adaptation and use of comparative advantage benefits from siting different stages of production in different locations. Operations can be sited in markets around the world, to take advantage of local comparative advantage in production, but extreme economies of scale are balanced with multiple production sites to incorporate regional tastes and to offer the potential for arbitraging among regions, all while keeping downstream activities close to the customer. As with other IO-based models, companies gain success from properly understanding their industries, then matching strategies to industry requirements.

The forces driving global competition

Prahalad, Doz, Porter, and their followers describe and discuss the kinds of industries that will lean toward global integration or towards responsiveness. George Yip developed a model that detailed what he has called globalization vs. responsiveness drivers in some detail.[8] Yip's four key driving forces are markets, costs, government, and competition. Depending on how it aligns with each (and all) of these drivers, any industry can be assessed for its relative potential for successful globalization. In his most recent update to this model, Yip notes that all drivers seem to be moving toward globalization across the board. Of course, this analysis addresses conditions prior to the current world economic downturn, but it does suggest that long-term trends seem to be in the direction of integration of markets and efficient use of resources.

Market drivers are tied to converging customer tastes and needs around the world – a trend that seems to be increasing constantly in the opinion of many observers. Similar customer demands allow firms to avoid adjusting their marketing mix from place to place. Global branding, an increasing trend, rewards transnational standardization with promises of world-class quality, technology, and price norms for customers anywhere. Likewise, firms that sell to other global firms have few pressures to change their products, while worldwide logistical nets, both for inputs and for distribution, encourage a focus on value and productivity rather than adaptation. Finally, rapid globalization of ICT through fiber optic cable, satellite communication, the Internet, and so forth, allow global firms to push their messages to consumers around the world – and from the top to ever closer to the bottom of the economic scale.

Cost drivers also are leaning ever more in favor of the global. Economies of scale and scope continue to grow, and the trend toward offshore production of both goods and services suggests that efforts to combine these economies with location-tied comparative advantage have been extremely successful. Improved logistics have made dispersed value-adding activities much more economical, so that even when some stages of the value-adding chain – final assembly, for instance – might be regional or local, many inputs come from a few global sources. Thus, the quintessentially American Apple iPhone is assembled in Taiwan from largely Asian-sourced parts designed by a wide range of American, European, and Japanese technology companies. Quality and technology from the best in the world, but costs held in line by equally world-class manufacturing in most productive locations. The costs of technology design in such a fast changing industry are helped by a global production system added to the global marketing of Apple's iconic products.

Government drivers have been moving toward the global for the past several decades. The expansion of the World Trade Organization (WTO), particularly the accession of China, has driven trade barriers to historic lows. Converging technical standards and intellectual property protection laws, influenced by industry and demand pressures in response to economic development that has moved innovation away from a strictly American-European Union-Japan axis, make the global supply network feasible. Even as bilateral squabbles over hormone-fed beef, pirated software, dumped steel and the like continue, technologically advanced industries experience much less disruption. This is the area, though, that may be most threatened by the current global economic downturn. As governments face rising unemployment, pressures to favor local workers in government-funded programs are also rising. So we see in early 2009 that the American bailout for industry has a "buy American" component, the French government is offering support to Peugeot and Renault in exchange for promises not to cut jobs in France, and

China is determined to support its export economy. Again, though, the focus seems to be on labor-intensive traditional industries, which are ever less important on the global stage.

Competitive drivers seem to favor globalization as well. More than ever, major firms from the Industrial Triad countries are succeeding in each other's home markets. Toyota has displaced General Motors as the largest auto company in the world, and is pressing hard to surpass GM even in North America. The largest banks are acquiring access to all the largest markets. Integration of the industrial markets continues on a path that dates back for decades. Of more note, though, we see the rise of ever more multinationals from emerging markets as serious global competitors. Indian steel companies (Tata and Mittal) are buying their way to global prominence, Tata Motors has bought Jaguar and Landrover from Ford, Ranbaxy Laboratories is moving beyond contract production of generic pharmaceuticals to develop its own independent R&D capacity, Lenovo from China has bought IBM's personal computer business, Haier is not only selling refrigerators in the US, but is looking for local brands to acquire, Embraer of Brazil is dominating the market for smaller regional jet aircraft. These and other examples suggest that even as more traditional multinational firms are moving to compete in ever more markets, ever more firms from around the world are aggressively entering the traditional advanced markets.

Yip's model suggests that globalization is advancing – though perhaps a bit more slowly at the moment – but more importantly it offers a systematic approach to industry analysis that can inform strategists about when they need to most consider international competition – and when they should most consider becoming global competitors. It emphasizes the risks of too short an analytic horizon for companies considering who are their competitors, who might be their competitors tomorrow, where new technologies might arise, and how far their logistical chains reach. It does not supplant other models of industry analysis, but provides considerable insight on how and how broadly to apply them.

Life cycles, local markets, and outsourcing

Industry conditions are not static conditions, but rather they evolve as technologies, markets, and firm competencies evolve. An early dynamic model of strategy was Raymond Vernon's International

Product Life Cycle (IPLC), mentioned in the previous chapter as an example of firms responding to evolving comparative advantage.[9] Developed as a descriptive model of the post-World War II world in which the United States controlled almost half the global economy, much of the rest of the industrial world had been battered or destroyed by war, and less developed countries were just beginning to emerge from colonial status, the IPLC proposed that new products would emerge initially in developed countries, usually the US, in response to local demand and technological development.

Initial production would be in the home market and would be based on skilled-labor intensive, highly specialized processes. Lower levels of demand in the rest of the world, largely from other industrial nations, would be satisfied by exports from the originating country. Over time, demand in the home country would tend to become saturated and the market would mature, while demand continued to develop in other industrial countries and to emerge in the less developed world, and production processes would tend to become standardized with experience. Production would move to lower cost locations as standardization allowed less skilled workers to function adequately, and increasing demand in less developed countries grew. Residual demand in the developed world would be satisfied by production in the less developed countries and reverse trade.

Finally, as the product matured, new products would tend to replace it in US and other industrial countries, so the demand would shift almost completely to the developing world. During the early phases of the IPLC, competition would be on product differentiation, but as the product and industry matured, competition would shift to a price basis, and efficient low cost production would become a key competency.

The IPLC seemed to collapse into a global product life cycle toward the end of the twentieth century, as previously underdeveloped nations developed more sophisticated demand, and Europe and Japan matched the development and technological sophistication levels of the US. However, the emergence of the big emerging markets in India, China, Russia, and perhaps Brazil has attracted investment to these countries both as offshore platforms and to satisfy relatively small, but rapidly growing, local demand. Thus, today we once again see major US technology firms shifting the production, and even the development, of more mature products to China and India both to lower costs at home and to offer competitive products in those countries. Offshoring reflects the same drive to reduce costs that powered the IPLC, but it is happening even while demand in industrial markets is still growing – even at the launch of some new technology-intensive products. Gradualism in market development and production economies has been replaced by globalization along the value-adding process.

Global Service Industries and E-Commerce

Most models of multinational strategy have been developed with manufacturing industries in mind. Of course, most models of strategy, even of business in general, have explicitly or tacitly focused on manufacturing industries. Concepts of economies of scale, product life cycles, competitive forces and so on are more apparently relevant in the step-by-step production of goods, where product development, production, distribution, marketing, and other value-adding processes are easily distinguishable. Services are more difficult to separate, describe, and model; yet as the industrial world has switched to largely service-based economies, this is obviously worth doing.

The traditional distinguishing characteristic of services has always been the idea that they are produced and consumed simultaneously – there is no logistical queuing. This seems to be generally true of personal services. Haircuts, restaurant meals, live entertainment, medical care, and other activities that require physical contact can be categorized in this way. However, many other services are delivered through various media, and are not actually produced and consumed simultaneously. Thus, most books, motion pictures, recorded music, software, and so forth are intermediary devices to move a service, whether entertainment or information, across time and space. The added value of a motion picture, for instance, is not the DVD on which it is recorded, worth a few cents at best, but the information recorded on it, the content. What we see is that most information-based services, and particularly professional services, are not actually produced and consumed simultaneously. Rather, the information is recorded on some medium, generally of low value in itself, transmitted across time and space, and reproduced on some (often expensive) equipment. The consequence is that service industries are often international industries and require multinational strategies.

Entertainment industries have long been transnational. Squabbles over the cultural content of American motion pictures,

British pop music, Japanese *manga* comics, and the like "invading" other nations have gone on for decades. French attempts to maintain language purity by limiting the availability of American pop culture and "Franglais" slang have outraged, bemused, and provided materials for international studies professors. Such cultural purity efforts seem to be much along the lines of holding back the tides. However, as described by Thomas Friedman in his book *The Lexus and the Olive Tree*,[10] local cultural efforts to limit the encroachments of globalized Western culture have, when combined with the very information technologies that spread that culture, led to disasters like the World Trade Center attacks and the deepening divide between traditionalist Islamic states and modernizing Western economies. Much of these cultural influences are spread by information-based service industries committed to selling entertainment, but collaterally spreading social and cultural messages. Service industries are creating great resistance to their own products among national institutions – even as demand for these products increases among individuals. At the same time, for some products in some countries – say software in China – demand that outstrips adequately priced supply has led to massive piracy of ideas with minimal governmental interference. Information provision can be done indirectly via various media, so it can and is done internationally to great profits, but also with considerable disruption of social, cultural, legal, and governmental institutions. In comparison, selling cars and computers appears fairly innocuous.

The big international strategy story of the last few years in the United States is business process offshoring. This is the process of locating the sourcing of business services in foreign countries, whether in wholly-owned facilities or through outsourcing contractors. This process has been around for a long time, in reality. American companies have long employed London-based investment banks and advertising firms to provide financial and marketing services for their value chains, and regional headquarters have long provided the administrative overhead services for foreign investments. As most of these activities were either reciprocated among the industrial countries (British firms used New York-based advertising firms, too), or were part of larger direct investment transactions that generated profits in foreign markets for repatriation, little was made of them. More recently, though, primarily domestic businesses, particularly in the United States, have discovered that many information-based business processes could be provided with more than adequate quality and skill and at a much lower cost by knowledge workers in India,

China, the Philippines, Mexico, and other emerging economies. Suddenly, service jobs were moving abroad to support the generation of domestic profits, not foreign investment. The much lower salaries and vast numbers of workers in these countries seemed to offer insatiable competition for domestic workers. And the low levels of development in these nations suggested that reciprocal job and value creation was unlikely in the reasonable future.

The key to these happenings is the information technology revolution. Worldwide fiber-optic cable networks, faster computers, the Internet, and the Worldwide Web, jet travel, cellular telephones, and other technological solutions to the problem of long delays in intercontinental communication have changed the terms of competition in service industries. Any service that is based on information as opposed to personal touch can be offered indirectly. Thus, computer help desks in India can provide simultaneous answers to consumers in the United States via satellite and fiber-optic connected telephone communications. Other workers in the same facility in Mumbai or Bangalore can provide payroll services for that computer company by receiving, processing, and returning files on Internet-connected computers. And today, others may be involved in writing new software to make these processes more efficient.

An important source of competitive advantage in service industries lies in figuring out ever finer divisions of value-adding activities so that information processing can be separated from personal contacts, turned into technology-supported activities, and sourced to the most productive provider, whether in-house or outsourced, domestic or international. Today, we even see the "back-office providers" based in India and China moving to set up their own front-office operations in the industrialized world, rather than just acting as information processors for the IBMs, Accentures, and Dells of the world. They have learned that the real profits in services are still tied to the interpersonal, as the informational side has become rapidly commoditized. The offshoring scare reached into American presidential politics in the 2004 election, but by the next election was already losing a bit of sting as rising salaries in India and China on the "high-tech" side of services, and new, high-paying, jobs in the US on the "high-touch" side (made possible only because of cost savings on the low value-added tech side) shift the value proposition back to the domestic market. Information technology improvements have made the provision of information technology a cost-driven, low value-adding, commodity service in what seems the blink of an eye. The value of services, including business processes, is shifting back to those with the skills and location to interact directly with customers, while the technologies that they represent enable them to offer far superior services at much lower costs through an international "virtual logistics system" for information. Amazing – and very much a competitive strategic situation.

SUMMARY

So we see that industry analysis is still critical in the globalizing world of international business. Indeed, as more and more industries, such as IT and business process provision, are created and separated from manufacturing and traditional service industries, just understanding what industry we are in is becoming a critical strategic concern. Standard industry analysis tools, such as the Five Forces Model or market segmentation, and measures, such as concentration ratios or relative bargaining power, are relevant in internationalized or globalized industries. Strategists must simply take a broader perspective, look to a wider horizon, in deciding who are their competitors. In addition, though, understanding aspects of international competition, such as pressures for global or regional integration and pressures for local adaptation, are somewhat unique to multinational strategies. Geographical dispersion of operations, customers, and competition requires the use of more tools for strategic analysis, the recognition of the larger scope and scale of industry and competition, and a greater tolerance for uncertainty and complexity than the same activities applied only in a domestic market. The same concerns apply to understanding the abilities and limitations of the firm, as we shall see in the next chapter.

Key Points in the Chapter

1 The tools of industry analysis are usable in the international marketplace, but must be applied with an eye to global competition and to the unique aspects of the international industry, not just to a local market – even a big one.

2 An international perspective on industries suggests that the characteristics of some industries reward the benefits of size – economies of scale, market power, and so forth – and drive competition to global efficiencies.

3 Other industries reward firms that can adapt their products to unique local demand characteristics – a lack of responsiveness will limit market potential.

4 In the process of simultaneously satisfying these competing demands, industries can be described as favoring either concentrated or dispersed configurations – that is, different degrees of internationalization of activities – and either independent or integrated operations – fewer or more cross-border ties of operations to take advantage of differences in local advantages.

5 Globalization seems to be driving ever more industries to compromise situations where low-value-adding operations are sited in low cost locations with global remits, while customer-focused activities are dispersed and local – but tied into a global strategy.

Notes

1 Porter, M.E. (1980) *Competitive Strategy: Techniques for Analyzing Industries and Competitors*. New York: The Free Press.

2 Subsequent academic studies have established that while industry has some influence on business-level performance, business and firm-level factors have greater explanatory power, but industry setting still matters to strategy analysis.

3 Porter, M.E. (1980) n. 1 above.

4 Porter, M.E. (1986) "Competition in global industries: a conceptual framework". In M.E. Porter (ed.) *Competition in Global Industries*. Boston, MA: Harvard Business School Press: 15–60.

5 Prahalad, C.K. and Doz, Y. (1987) *The Multinational Mission: Balanc-ing Local Demands and Global Vision*. New York: The Free Press.

6 Bartlett, C.A. and Ghoshal, S. (1989) *Managing Across Borders: The Transnational Solution*. Boston: The Free Press.

7 Porter (1986) n. 4 above.

8 Yip, G.S. (2003) *Total Global Strategy II*. Upper Saddle River, NJ: Pearson Education International.

9 Vernon, R. (1966) "International investments and international trade in the product life cycle", *Quarterly Journal of Economics*, May: 190–207.

10 Friedman, T.L. (1999) *The Lexus and the Olive Tree*. New York: Farrar, Straus, and Giroux.

CHAPTER 5
Firm-specific Resources and Capabilities in the Global Setting

Strategy in Action

For decades now, Toyota Motor Corporation has been the most efficient auto manufacturer worldwide in terms of average labor hours required per unit of production. This condition generally is attributed to the success of the Toyota Production System (TPS), the complex combination of just-in-time logistics, close coordination with suppliers, total quality management, continuous improvement, and other systematic approaches to maximizing production efficiency. This system not only produces cars with great efficiency, but also produces some of the most reliable vehicles ever known from Toyota and Lexus. Before Toyota began production in North America, its success was attributed by the American Big Three producers and the United Auto Workers (UAW) union to its low labor costs and Japanese workers. However, in its NUMMI joint venture with General Motors and then in several wholly-owned production plants, Toyota showed that its process models could be applied with equal success to American workers in an American industrial environment (though one in which locations were chosen for their right-to-work laws and weak union traditions to avoid organizing by the UAW).

The TPS has been written about in a variety of books and many articles; Toyota has been open in permitting visitors and researchers, including those from its competitors, to tour its facilities; it has managed a joint venture with its primary worldwide competitor according to its system, including providing detailed training to GM managers and technicians; and most of its component systems are widely known and copied in many industries. Its major Japanese competitors, such as Nissan, Honda, Mazda, and Mitsubishi, have copied many of its approaches with considerable success, but without the single-minded devotion that would be needed to actually match Toyota's success. American and Japanese firms have tried to apply various parts of the TPS with a degree of success and some, such as the Saturn division of GM, have pursued a Toyota-like production system of their own (in Saturn's case, based largely on corporate experience in NUMMI).

Lower cost vehicles are made in China, Malaysia, or India thanks to much lower labor costs, but Toyota is also becoming an important presence in these markets. The widespread and continuing success of the TPS in the face of tough competition and inveterate imitation – with considerable understanding of how the TPS works – shows how complex capabilities can become and remain core competencies over long periods. As the competition closes in, Toyota continues to invest in and refine its systems, adapt them to new markets from the most advanced to the most underdeveloped, and to remain as the efficiency and reliability champion. Over time, across markets, and in a variety of models and sectors of the transportation industry, Toyota has been able to apply its set of complex, deeply embedded, team-based, and ever-refined skills to sustain competitive advantage against all comers. This is competitive advantage through capabilities.

Firm-specific Resources and Capabilities

As we have seen, from a resource-based perspective firms gain and maintain sustainable competitive advantage from their internalization of unique, firm-specific strategic resources. Barney[1] lists physical, human, and organizational resources, but with a focus on unique organizational resources, also described as capabilities or core competencies,[2] as the primary sources of sustained advantage, because physical and human resources are more easily compromised. Because such capabilities are defined as complex, organizationally embedded, shared knowledge of organizational processes, they are the epitome of valuable (they describe how a particular complex organization is operated); rare (based on experience and evolutionary processes, capabilities are essentially unique to individual organizations); difficult to imitate (their complexity and evolutionary nature make copying capabilities impossible); and difficult to substitute (while all organizations have their own processes, the successful applications that constitute capabilities may be partially substituted by alternative processes, but the outcomes will never be identical). From a resource-based perspective, then, the majority of successful international strategies come from building and exploiting complex organizational knowledge systems, and this will be the focus of the chapter.

However, it is notable that firms may be able to defend physical and human resources more successfully in international markets than in a single domestic market. Even natural resources, because they are unevenly distributed across the Earth, can become sustainable sources of advantage for those firms that are granted access to them, if supported by sophisticated political strategies that use government restrictions to protect firms' property rights from competition. Diamonds, copper, tin, even petroleum, are all found in limited locations and access is largely granted by national governments in most of the world. Political resources are also of considerable importance internationally. Access to inputs and markets, barriers to competitors, the influence of regulatory bodies – all these and other important aspects of the legal and regulatory environment can be used to gain competitive advantage by the firm with strong political resources. In the past, financial resources have also offered sustained advantage, but as financial markets around the world have become more integrated and more efficient, having access to financing is less of a differentiating factor for multinational firms when competing against each other, although it can still offer some advantage against local competitors in emerging markets where financing is still difficult.

In this chapter, we will first consider the how, what, and why of resources and capabilities as the bases of competitive advantage for a firm. Then we will consider how firms might build capabilities in their home markets that allow them to differentiate themselves for sustained competitive advantage in the international marketplace. Finally, we will consider how firms might build new capabilities in individual foreign markets and in the global marketplace itself.

Resources, Capabilities, and Competitive Advantage

From a business strategy view, its resources and capabilities are the sources of internal strengths and weaknesses for a firm. Exploiting the unique resources and capabilities that the firm *does* possess is the basis for profitability, growth, and other aspects of competitive success. Building up stores of resources and capabilities that the firm does *not* have in adequate supply works to correct the competitive weaknesses that keep the firm from matching its competitors. While the strategic resources and capabilities that make a firm successful must be unique or rare in order to generate advantage at any given time, this is not a permanent condition – resources decay, capabilities decline, competitors find their own new sources of advantage, and the market shifts away from the products of older capabilities. Thus, the basic strategic requirements in this perspective are exploiting resources and capabilities to gain market success and building stocks of resources and capabilities to maintain competitive advantage into the future.

Identifying strengths – firm-specific resources and capabilities to exploit

All firms, to include multinationals, need an awareness of what they own, control, or can access that makes them special – their strengths or strategic resources and capabilities. Not all complex capabilities are necessarily easy to understand or to pin down exactly, but firms can still understand how their particular skills and methods work for them. In identifying sources of competitive advantage, perhaps the most important item to remember is the customer. Products are only valuable if the customer is willing to pay for them, and resources and capabilities are only valuable if they enable the firm to make or to do things that are of value to its customers. If what we do does not enable our customers to either reduce their costs or to offer greater value to *their* customers, we will not be able to charge a premium. So let's look at how resources and capabilities figure in this system.

Physical Resources – As we have said, physical resources are often seen as offering only temporary competitive advantage. Locations can be copied – how often is a K-Mart found right next to a Wal-Mart in the US? Patents can be licensed or invented around – once engineers know that a product *can* be made, they *will* find a way. Our new clean room facility can be supplanted by theirs – with suitable upgrades to make us obsolete once again. Multinational firms, however, do at times find more sustainable advantages in their physical resources. Natural resource-based companies typically can only access their raw materials in a limited number of locations – often in foreign countries. Companies that can win concessions from the local government can often maintain possession, or at least control, over mines, wells, quarries, and the like for extended periods, and entry into the industry is not possible without a source of supply. Of course, strong political capabilities are useful in conjunction with strong sources of physical resources, as it is often political favoritism that provides protected access at below-market rates.

Thus, a copper mine in a free market situation should be valued just at the net present value of its expected earnings, so a company must either have owned the mine for many years or have a low-cost process technology, for it will pay the previous owner for all its expected future earnings. However, in less open political and economic situations, a firm might be able to acquire and retain its rights to inputs at below market rates through political interests or other non-market means, to include gifts and bribes, illegal though they might be. By accessing unique physical assets, then tying them up through government connections or simply because they are too remote for many competitors to be interested, firms gain advantage.

Human Resources – As we have seen, human resources can be of great value – a few key scientists and engineers tend to make most of the important discoveries for a firm – but can be difficult to sustain. Once an individual recognizes his or her own value, he or she can leave the firm for a better paying position, often with a competitor, start his or her own business, or just threaten to do so and force the company to pay his true worth. Since this is the present value of the expected cash flows generated by that individual's activities, this can severely hamper the firm's ability to profit from unique individuals. The company does better when value is generated by teams of individuals, particularly teams of fairly ordinary individuals inspired by their organization rather than their own genius. Again, though, multinationals may be able to gain more sustainable advantage from their access to talented individuals than can domestic firms in advanced economies by exploiting their skills at finding and managing resources in multiple locations. By tapping highly skilled individuals in less developed markets, then exploiting their discoveries in the developed market economies, multinational firms can profit.

So, teams of mathematicians in Bulgaria, software writers in Russia, machine operators in China, or call center operators in India can be paid more than their market value in their home countries, but much less than their potential real value in an advanced market. So long as the individuals cannot relocate and other firms do not enter the foreign market to bid up salaries, the multinational can maintain a cost advantage over domestic rivals in its home market. Indeed, the ability to access and exploit human resources in such fashion is the basis of the current trends in outsourcing services. If an Indian radiologist can read an x-ray equally as well as, and thanks to digital technology, equally as quickly as an American one, then a company employing the Indian will have a competitive advantage. Of course, in the recent past that Indian radiologist would have sought to emigrate to the US or Western Europe and today many other hospital groups are bidding for his services in Bangalore or Mumbai, but until he is paid his full value in the developed market, adjusted perhaps for risk and access costs, multinational hospital groups will maintain their advantage over domestic ones. So, even in foreign markets human resources tend to have limited value as sources of sustained advantage for their employees, but they are more sustainable internationally than in developed markets.

Organizational Resources – Physical resources are relatively easy to imitate and human resources compete for value share – employees can always walk or shirk if they feel that they are not maximizing their personal gain. As sources of sustainable advantage *for the firm*, neither is a long-term reliable asset. What the multinational firm needs are firm-specific resources and capabilities (FSRCs). These are knowledge resources that are tied to the organization, not to any of its component parts. Such resources tend to be tacit (an understanding, not codified knowledge), path-dependent (based on experience), organizationally embedded (group knowledge that is not destroyed by the coming and going of individual employees), complex (consisting of multiple bits of knowledge), and so generating advantage from somewhat ambiguous sources. At their simplest, such resources are often referred to as *routines*, or standardized ways of performing certain tasks that develop among groups of people engaged in a set of activities.[3] *Capabilities* are more complex sets of routines that guide people in an organization in performing complicated operations in the most efficient manner. *Core competencies* are capabilities that are tied closely to the economic identity of the firm, the things that are the basis for the unique aspects of the company, and that can be applied to multiple businesses within the firm.[4] *Dynamic capabilities* are capabilities for adapting the firm's competencies to a changing situation that evolve (or co-evolve, to use the current term) with the ever-changing industrial environment of the firm.[5] Finding or creating such firm-specific dynamic capabilities is the essence of resource-based strategy.

An example of an organizational capability is the Toyota Production System described at the start of the chapter. This combination of Total Quality Management, just-in-time logistics, continual improvement, and a variety of other production management techniques has made Toyota the most efficient automotive producer for decades. Despite its widespread recognition, other manufacturers have struggled to incorporate the various parts of the system. Even General Motors, which has had direct access to the joint facility that the two firms operate in California, has been unable to replicate and sustain anything approaching Toyota's efficiency in its own facilities. Other MNEs have developed institutional systems for managing strategic moves such as acquisitions or alliances, for managing knowledge flows internally, or for entering foreign markets. While harder to associate with specific performance improvements, capabilities for effectively and efficiently managing complex general management issues can be of particular value to firms. McKinsey's knowledge management system, Hewlett-Packard's system for organizing internal alliances, or GE's approach to acquisition and disposal of subsidiaries are often noted examples.

Supporting strengths – complementary and co-specialized resources

Resource-based strategy concepts may place competitive advantage with the control of property rights to firm-specific resources and capabilities, but that does not necessarily mean that simple possession of FSRCs always generates economic benefits. Rather, these assets must be deployed strategically in order to generate products based on the FSRCs and deliver them to customers. To do so, the truly unique FSRCs of a firm must often be surrounded and supported by an array of less idiosyncratic assets. First, firms must have adequate access to the most basic of resources – capital, facilities, human resources, and other fungible inputs. While these resources only generate unique outputs when organized into specialized capabilities or put to work on a unique design, without them, the firm cannot function. Though in theory any project with a positive net present value should be funded, many an entrepreneur who has not found funding knows that the best ideas often fail to launch due to the lack of capital. For multinational firms, particularly those operating in foreign countries with non-market economies (or strong government involvement in a supposed market), ability to access land, labor, and local capital can be – or become – problematic. Thus, local party bosses in China or government authorities in India – or their counterparts in many locations – can restrict, delay, or deny access to commodities in order to enhance their own influence, solicit payments, or limit foreign influences in some locations.

Even when firms can access marketable resources, they may need more specialized – but what are not truly unique or restricted – resources and capabilities to get products into the market place. Thus, EMI from Britain introduced the first CT scanner and built a solid market and production base in its home market. As EMI attempted to enter the US market for medical devices, though, General Electric came out with a competing product. Even though the GE scanner was technically no better, or even less capable, than the EMI product, the distribution system, personal relationships, and brand name of this major competitor in the US enabled GE to rapidly dominate the US market for CT scanners and eventually to buy up EMI's operation.[6] The sort of resources and capabilities brought to bear by GE in this case are referred to as complementary resources. Typically the type of organizational skills such as distribution or marketing that are not inherently unique, but which provide necessary support for fully exploiting unique products, complementary resources are essential to creating superior value. However, these resources need not be owned – they are often sourced from specialists through extended contracts and other alliance mechanisms. Thus, advertising is often handled by specialist firms even for the largest manufacturing companies. Local distribution, particularly in foreign markets, is often handled by local firms – and even global logistics are handled more and more by freight forwarding and logistics specialists. These firms, by specializing in distribution, can deliver a unique product to the right customer more efficiently and accurately than can the originating firm. To the manufacturer, these are complementary capabilities. Unless the product *can* be delivered, it has no value to the customer, no matter how perfect it might be, so the quality of this service is essential. However, the act of delivery is a cost, not a source of value, to the manufacturer, and is best handled through the market.

If complementary resources are adapted to a specific use in order to better support the rent-generating capacity of the firm's specialized resources and capabilities, they lose their generic capacity to support other opportunities. They adjust – or are adjusted – to better complement the FSRCs in the specific situation to gain improved efficiency. We say that they have become co-specialized resources, valuable in a particular use, but of much less value in other situations.

Home Country Advantage and the Origins of FSRCs

John Dunning[7] says that the ownership advantages of multinational enterprises derive from conditions in their home countries. Michael Porter's[8] view of the competitive advantage of nations is that the national "diamond of competitive advantage" allows the firms from countries with the right combinations of resource endowments, industry competition, supporting industries and institutions, and consumer demand to enter the international marketplace with strategic advantages over other multinationals from, and local firms in, less advantaged locations. However, Alan Rugman[9] clearly distinguishes between country-specific advantage (CSA) and firm-specific advantage (FSA). "Country-specific advantage" and "the competitive advantage of nations" are constructs that apply the notion of national comparative advantage from Chapter 3 to the specific assets and skills of individual companies based in those nations. This is the idea that location provides advantage to firms located in that place – region or country. However, the concept of FSRCs or FSAs goes a bit farther and suggests that firms develop internally particular bundles of resources and capabilities in the process of competing in their home markets that can persist beyond the boundaries of their home location.

Strong firms tend to reflect the markets of their home countries. Discussions of national comparative advantage (Chapter 3) can be related to the interests and skills of firms from a given country. We would not expect strong gas and oil drilling, service, or refining firms from Japan, for instance, where there are virtually no petroleum resources. We would expect Japanese companies to excel in miniaturization, personal electronics, and other technologies and industries that would be supported by a large, concentrated, and sophisticated population, just as we might expect American firms to excel at labor-saving technologies (the US had the most expensive work force in the industrial world for decades after World War II) and communication technology (large domestic distances). Besides industry sector focus, home-based conditions can drive firms to strengthen their competitive skills, as Porter shows with his diamond model. Thus, sophisticated local demand, strong competition, good supporting institutions and industries, and resource conditions that add pressure to competition all work to refine the competitive capabilities of firms in ways that go beyond traditional comparative advantage. The competitive advantage of nations is really about the combined competitive advantage of national firms. For the best firms, such advantage is internalized and converted into FSRCs as these companies become multinationals. The somewhat mysterious development of firm-specific resource and capability pools can be attributed at least in part to the comparative and competitive advantages of their home markets. However, much of the firm-specific advantage of multinational firms comes from FSRCs that are developed and exploited in international markets.

Clusters, city regions, and FSRCs

What makes international strategy different is its focus on location as a key part of the strategic equation. The name of the field ties it closely to national identity – both home and host markets. However, the focus of location-based strategy is moving away from countries as the key unit of analysis toward much smaller geographical spaces. Economic geography since the beginning of the twentieth century has identified industrial districts from England to Northern Italy to Southern Germany, and now in the United States, China, and virtually every other place that has been considered. Business strategy has begun to absorb the idea that location-tied sources of advantage are based in much more tightly defined areas than those described by national boundaries. Michael Porter has become a primary proponent of the idea that competitive advantage largely arises in these small, homogenous communities of co-located and commercially tied firms.[10] Others have taken a slightly more conceptual approach to what have been called "global city regions".[11] This terminology recognizes that most of the world's economic output is focused in a relatively small number of major metropolitian areas around the globe. Each of these mega-cities may contain a number of industrial clusters, but they also provide the essential physical, institutional, and human infrastructure to support a variety of industries, both as markets and as sources of goods and services.

From the perspective of the multinational firm, these ideas mean that companies do not invest in China, but in Shanghai or Guangdong, not in the USA, but in Silicon Valley or the Research Triangle, not in the EU, or even in France, but in Strasbourg or Lyon. Entry into national markets is often through the gateway of a major city region, or even a specific industry cluster – the local knowledge of a specific market is concentrated in these places. Even more important, though, given today's expanding global value chains, is the importance of these clusters as reservoirs of knowledge about an industry sector. The evidence suggests that most innovation in most industries is concentrated in such clusters, and when multinational firms look to other countries for offshore sites for production, research and development, or business support, they are most likely to maximize their benefits by locating inside the right clusters in the right cities. Thus, even as costs rise and workers become more difficult to attract and retain, companies from around the world still look to Bangalore, India as a site for IT support or Shanghai as a place for outsourced manufacturing. The value of a knowledgeable, experienced workforce, nearby suppliers, specialized universities, government encouragement, and competitors to learn from, all make these places prime locations in which to gain the resources and capabilities to compete on an equal basis worldwide.

Of course, clusters have disadvantages, too. Evidence exists that the most innovative multinationals tend to avoid clusters when investing in a foreign country, most likely to avoid situations in which they lose more knowledge to spillovers than they can gain.[12] Of course, these firms often come from clusters in their own home countries, and are likely seeking markets more than new knowhow. Nevertheless, evidence suggests that firms in clusters generate more knowledge, or at least patents, than do isolated firms, but that they are less likely to produce blockbuster patents. Other studies suggest that over time clusters tend to become inward-focused, ever better at the same things, while the world moves on elsewhere. Cluster-tied firms end up in capability traps that catch an entire population, not just a single firm.[13] Still, the idea that foreign direct investment should be targeted much more carefully than simply looking for the least costly site in the right country has considerable power. Perhaps multinational firms do not need to place every plant in a hot spot of innovation for their respective industries, but they do need to bear in mind that when they want to tap the sources of new ideas, they must consider the benefits of entering a cluster along with its limitations.

Resources, Capabilities, and Multinational Strategies[14]

Industrial organization models of strategy look to industry characteristics to explain performance, and anticipate oligopolistic relationships among the small number of successful incumbent firms in the industry. However, a variety of studies have shown that industry membership is not a major factor in explaining differences in performance across firms. Rather, differences in performance from business to business within an industry are much greater than differences between diversified corporations or industries.[15] This strongly supports the core proposition of resource-based strategy, that unique firm-specific explanatory factors – assets and capabilities – explain the majority of differences in performance. This model can be quite compatible with Porter's model of industry, if we recognize that each firm in an industry is unique and will follow its own strategy. Industry provides a setting for strategy and the competition that puts evolutionary pressures on the firm.

Strategies from the resource-based perspective fulfill two main roles – resource exploitation for the purpose of earning rents (gaining competitive advantage) to the firm's unique assets and capabilities and resource-building for the purpose of renewing and increasing assets and capabilities for sustained competitive advantage. These strategies can be pursued by multinational firms through both internationalization and through global integration. These are the same generic international strategies that support matching industry demands, matching competitive with comparative advantage and so forth. The consideration here is that resource-based strategy focuses on the internal competencies of the firm, rather than on its positioning in the external marketplace – a difference of focus, but not one that requires a different set of responses (though it may offer alternative solutions to the same apparent problems!) David Collis introduced resource-based concepts from resource-based theory (core competencies and firm capabilities in his terminology) to the study of the multinational firm in his study of the bearings industry, adding path dependency constraints on choice and the existence of complex capabilities as sources of unique advantage to the four rules described above.[16] Bruce Kogut explicitly incorporates evolutionary considerations into a first attempt to describe a new model of the multinational firm, although more from an international business than a strategic perspective,[17] and Gunnar Hedlund and Johan Ridderstrale use dynamic capabilities theory to address organizational issues in multinationals. They describe previous models of the multinational firm as focused on "... the exploitation of givens, rather than the creation of novelty".[18] They propose that both exploitation and creation are essential to a successful multinational strategy, yet they discuss them as diametrically opposed strategies. This section addresses how multinationals might pursue one or both of these imperatives of a capabilities-based, sustainable multinational strategy.

For the multinational firm developing and pursuing a strategy in the international arena, organizational capabilities present two major strategic imperatives. First, for the firm with existing unexploited or slack resources, expansion into international markets and integration across these markets provide new opportunities to derive additional rents from existing capabilities, that is, capability leverage. Resource-based or capability-based models see international expansion as providing a wide scope for the exploitation of existing assets and skills to increase rents to core technologies while reducing competitive risks, and to compete more successfully with local and international competitors. This vision of multinational strategy provides an interpretation of international activity that is compatible with traditional and industrial organization models, but with a micro-analytical focus. Global integration permits the multinational firm to exploit local comparative advantage efficiently, to leverage its bargaining power across markets, and to arbitrage cost differentials effectively.[19] Evidence indicates that firms which have developed divisional structures for domestic product diversification can leverage these organizational competencies into multinational organization forms, suggesting that the key skill of transferring knowledge throughout a complex organization can be the basis for multinational expansion.[20]

Second, international expansion and global integration provide opportunities to create or build new FSRCs through exposure to new markets, internalization of new concepts, ideas from new cultures, access to new resources, and exposure to new competitors and terms of competition which can turn the multinational firm into a pluralistic rather than nationalistic entity. The availability of organizational capabilities for change and learning is the key to sustained success for multinational firms.[21] International opportunities can result (intentionally or not) in organizational learning and in building new capabilities that may be applicable to both old and new locations, and thus to the evolution of the firm's strategic configuration. The ability to transfer or arbitrage tacit, or difficult to codify, knowledge to widely scattered operations appears to be a major source of advantage for multinational firms.[22] From a capability-building perspective, firms can tap regional clusters in other countries either through acquisition of or alliance with a cluster member or through a startup in a highly advantaged region.[23] For example, we see a variety of foreign firms in the semiconductor and software industries locating in Silicon Valley in order to be close to the world center of innovation in these industries. Multinationals are no longer limited to competitive advantages developed back in the home market, but can uncover and incorporate new capabilities and resources abroad. These new and traditional approaches to the multinational firm suggest that existing assets and capabilities can be leveraged and enhanced through greater international presence.

Capability leverage strategies and the multinational firm

Leveraging existing resources and capabilities suggests certain pressures on the multinational firm as it devises its strategy. First, leverage alone implies static sources of advantage based on FSRCs derived from the home market. International markets represent opportunities to further leverage assets and capabilities which have been successfully exploited in the home market. Worldwide markets emphasize scale efficiency-focused capabilities while multi-domestic markets emphasize skills in flexible design, smaller scale production, sales, and marketing capabilities. Second, a preference for whole ownership is implied to protect these capabilities from prying partners and to permit the maximum strategic freedom to apply them in the "approved" manner – static advantage must emphasize preservation. Third, big companies are generally implied, as they have the managerial and financial assets to build an organization of wholly-owned subsidiaries over time and the existing market power to move product on the basis of low price while fighting to counter imitative competition. Fourth, home-based new product development is also implied, as this provides the best protection for skills in research and design. Foreign subsidiaries engaged in a corporate leverage strategy may modify home market designs given new knowledge about their host markets, but learning is very much in the "exploitative learning" mode[24] – the subsidiaries are learning to do better what the multinational firm already does.

The consequence of these strategic and structural characteristics of capability leverage strategies is that they result primarily in internationalization and globalization of markets, not globalization of strategy. Firms expand their market access and their dependency on international markets. They may well move operations abroad. They may organize into global or regional product divisions as their product lines supersede international boundaries. They may become large and powerful multinational firms, and may even sell similar product lines around the world, but in the absence of a competence-building, organizational learning-focused multinational strategy, they will not be truly global. What we can see clearly is that leverage or exploitative strategies are in line with the expectations of both industrial organization and transaction cost-based models that multinational firms primarily operate to extend home-based advantage into international markets. Whether looking to strategic maneuvering or to internalization to extend and protect competitive advantage, both concepts look to home markets as the sources of advantage and are largely concerned with exploiting and protecting existing sources of advantage in foreign markets. We also see why regional market expansion is so prevalent,[25] as FSRCs sourced from the home market are likely to be best exploited in nearby foreign markets.

Capability leverage and internationalization   Most studies of international diversification look to leveraging capabilities across more national markets as the key to economic success. Resource-based theory suggests that the same benefits of shared capabilities should occur across national markets as across product markets,[26] and transaction cost theory provides a strong argument for competitive advantage based on internal expansion by multinational firms.[27] Multinational firms with profit-making FSRCs will seek additional profits in international market locations, whether through exports, licensing, or direct investment. If these resources and capabilities are such that they are embedded in the firm's structure, these international markets will be internalized by foreign direct investment, ensuring the best application of the capabilities while protecting them from compromise.[28] So long as the FSRCs can be applied profitably, greater international market presence should generate higher performance levels. Thus, Toyota has been able to profit by selling cars made in Japan around the world, but also by building cars using the TPS in various countries from the United States to Thailand, and by allying with other firms, as in the case of the NUMMI joint venture with General Motors in California. Multinational firms that stay in their same product lines as they spread into new markets would seem able to leverage at least some of their unique capabilities in any national market, despite the need to adjust to local environmental factors. On the other hand, multinational expansion is difficult and complex and greater international dispersion must lead to the increased bureaucratic costs, limiting the scope of benefits to strategic resources internationally – at some point a firm may well become too large and complex to operate efficiently.

Empirical studies have produced a variety of results when looking at the profitability of international expansion. Grant, Jammine, and Thomas found that increased multinationalism among British MNEs improved accounting performance.[29] Geringer, Beamish, and DaCosta and others suggested a weak curvilinear response of performance to increased international spread.[30] However, when variables such as firm size, national identity, or industry characteristics are introduced as controls, the significance of the effect of international diversification on performance tends to be reduced.[31] As with product diversification, results are not always positive,[32] but the different measures used to describe geographical diversification also are not necessarily related to each other, effects may vary across different dependent variables, direction of investment flow may represent very different strategic purposes, and contextual differences such as exchange rates or economic performance can have a profound impact on the result of diversification.[33] For instance, Delios and Beamish[34] and Geringer, Tallman, and Olsen[35] found that increased international operations among Japanese multinationals led to increasing sales and lower profitability – but that these outcomes varied over time. So the negative effects of external conditions and of bureaucratic costs may well temper the rent-earning potential of international expansion.

Capability leverage and integration Leverage is enhanced by integrating markets. The ability to manage extensive networks of international subsidiaries at low transactional cost seems to be a key capability and source of sustainable competitive advantage for successful multinational firms.[36] Not only are existing capabilities extended to foreign markets, they are applied to a world market. Given the need to adapt somewhat to local differences, core FSRCs that can be targeted at regional or global markets gain maximum benefits to size and market strength. The multi-plant problem applied globally permits each process technology to be pushed to its limit, global products provide the returns needed to push technology and quality as far as possible, and brand names take on a larger-than-life aura. In addition to scope advantages, Kogut describes advantages of being able to arbitrage across markets, bargain more effectively in multiple markets, and leverage advantages from one market into others.[37] A company with an integrated network of production facilities can shift its efforts to take advantage of temporary currency effects, counter union pressures on wages, or transfer new technology from one location to another. Hamel and Prahalad focus on global brands, distribution capabilities, and leverage of financial resources across markets, all assets that can be leveraged within an integrated network of subsidiaries, as hallmarks of global strategy.[38]

Evidence suggests that managing a product-diversified firm can be leveraged into managing an internationally diversified firm.[39] Management capabilities, as well as technical skills, can be brought from national to international to global competition through extension and exploitative, efficiency-oriented learning. On the other hand, studies show that excessive bureaucratic costs associated with extremes of multinational expansion (and possibly global integration – the two are not easily separated in studies) will cause the performance of MNEs to fall off as diversification exceeds some intermediate level. Exactly what degree of diversification will cause bureaucratic costs to outstrip the cost economies and revenue enhancements due to more extensive exploitation of FSRCs requires an empirical answer, and one that likely varies from case to case. Certainly, though, global integration adds to the bureaucratic costs of multinational firms over an international holding company format. As large sample studies observe only levels of diversity of activities and related performance, but cannot easily address issues of strategic intent or management control structure, the value of global integration has not been well supported. Johansson and Yip use interview data to compare small samples of Japanese and American firms in a structural equation model of industry drivers and globalization strategies, finding that global strategy and structure affect the performance of US firms more than that of Japanese firms, but have positive impacts in both cases.[40]

Capability-building strategies and the multinational firm

In addition to leveraging their existing capabilities, most long-term successful multinational firms also build capabilities through their international operations, an essential activity if the firm is to have assets and capabilities to leverage on a continuing basis.[41] Dynamic capabilities suggest a process of interaction between firm-level initiatives and environmental pressures. These result in evolutionary strategies, by which companies either develop new FSRCs in response to a changing environment, or they will eventually lose out to selection pressures and fail. Thus, to stay with our auto industry example, we have seen the standardization strategy of General Motors supplanted by the quality and efficiency model of Toyota, which is pressured by a renewed focus on manufacturing in low-cost locations with global exports in the light of reduced trade barriers.

As in the case of leverage strategies, certain consequences for the strategic configuration of the multinational firm can be drawn from the demands of competence-building. First, advantage becomes dynamic, based on ability to create new, not to exploit old, capabilities. This implies the extensive use of joint ventures, alliances, and acquisitions to explore for new knowledge rather than a focus on whole ownership to protect old knowledge. Second, as technical capabilities can best be developed where the local "diamond" favors them,[42] a global search for new products and processes suggests product divisions based around the world, not based just in the home country. Third, capabilities must be shared, both inside and outside the firm, to make use of them before new learning makes them obsolete and to bring them together with other essential skills. This implies that internal networks are critical, providing a much more active role for the central headquarters and the need for active cooperation and routines to promote it. If differentiated networks are indeed the organizational structure of the global firm, then managerial capabilities for running complex organizations become sources of rents as well as drivers of internalization.[43] Thus, fourth, managing capabilities is as important to rent-earning as developing them, suggesting that central management functions may be value-enhancing, not value-destroying, as seems the case in many descriptions of diversified firms. However, the dispersed and decentralized nature of value-creating activities suggests that central management is more a matter of facilitating communication and cooperation among subsidiaries in a "heterarchy" than directing operations through the command and control model of a hierarchy.[44] Rather than finding such skills in international markets, the global MNE must generate them internally through processes of variation, identification, testing, and retention. To a large extent, the above suggests that the characteristics of successful leverage strategies create barriers to building innovative strategies, an implication borne out in most of the globalization literature. Understanding the nature of this anomaly and its possible solutions is perhaps the major issue in global strategy at this time. The most interesting new models of the MNE, such as dynamic capabilities models and evolutionary models, are concerned in great part with resolving the building–exploiting conundrum of global strategy.[45]

Capability-building and internationalization   If capability leverage strategies seem most intensely related to international expansion, capability-building among multinational firms appears to be

more closely tied to globalization efforts. However, internationalization certainly provides access to new products, processes, and technologies which can be incorporated into the firm's array of technical
competencies. No one country or region has the secret to technology. Many firms have come to the US seeking technical skills to
either outsource or incorporate in the search for international competitive advantage, and, indeed, US-based firms are discovering the
same technological capacities in European, East Asian, even former
socialist countries – highly skilled Russian computer programmers
have been used by Western industry for 10 years. Global multinationals encourage major new businesses to develop in the most
demanding foreign local markets where these technologies are most
advanced. A good bit of this learning is likely to be exploitative, in
the sense that the international firm is most likely to acquire capabilities and assets which are related to its existing resources. The role of
the multinational firm in acquiring new skills and transmitting them
to other units is challenged by the differences across markets. Even
in relatively recent writings, home country-derived tacit knowledge
is treated as the strength of the firm.[46] However, as the value of regional clusters of highly skilled firms to the development of knowledge has become more apparent, the possibilities for MNEs to learn
significant new capabilities, not just locally exploitable knowhow,
has given international spread a much greater role in knowledge
asset development. Such activities imply an openness to entirely
new constructs which is not a part of traditional models, whether
based on market power or internalization, of the multinational firm.
Ultimately, they also require a level of integration of knowledge
generating and knowledge using operations that is far beyond that
necessary to traditional MNEs.

Capability-building and globalization   It is through global integration that corporations appear to have the best chance to develop
knowledge resources and build new capabilities in international
markets. New models propose that the integrated global firm can
find technical and managerial knowhow in foreign locations which
would otherwise not be available to the firm, and then bring them
into the broader set of company skills to build new corporate capabilities. As Nohria and Ghoshal have it, "... a key advantage of the
multinational arises from its ability to create new value through the
accumulation, transfer, and integration of different kinds of knowledge, resources, and capabilities across its dispersed organizational

units".[47] Studies point to organizational learning effects from complex domestic organizations that might be applicable to international organizations. How much greater would the learning be from direct experiences in international markets? The existence of such learning is the basic assumption of Bartlett and Ghoshal's Transnational Firm and related models.[48] Organizational learning and development of organizational capabilities among multinationals suggest that the negative effects of bureaucratic costs overcome the benefits of multinational strategies and organization only in the extreme. These studies and others show that global integration provides global scope for search and recombination opportunities in creating new technology, and that operating a global network organization develops new management capabilities that inexperienced MNEs or domestic firms simply do not possess. Building capabilities through globalization is as much a creative process as an accumulative process. Simply gathering knowledge from various locations provides some value, but real rent-generating capacity requires the combination of this knowledge with old firm-level understandings on a much broader scale.

The empirical evidence of the advantages of capability-building for organizational performance is limited and largely anecdotal. However, even early models of gradual internationalization were based on observations of learning by gradual expansion and increasing competition in international markets.[49] Kogut and Zander show that the internal transfer of uncodifiable – or difficult to standardize and record – knowledge is typical of multinationals, inferring that the primary role of the multinational firm is knowledge transfer.[50] David Collis finds that while a strong heritage of national characteristics is carried by MNEs, continuous improvement on all dimensions of strategy is essential to long-term competitive advantage.[51] The case observations of Bartlett and Ghoshal and the more detailed studies presented by Nohria and Ghoshal show multinationals building new capabilities for competing successfully on a global scale, albeit starting from a nationally based administrative heritage.[52,53] Observation suggests a sea change in global strategy over the last decade or so from a focus on exploitative strategy with ancillary learning to a conscious and clearly expressed strategy among top multinational firms of seeking new products, processes, and capabilities around the world and moving these throughout the many integrated operations of the firm as rapidly as possible. We see Microsoft building software research facilities in China, first to pursue character-based systems for local use, but now (having learned about the Chinese environment and worker competencies) to develop code for worldwide use.

SUMMARY

Integrating capability exploitation and capability-building both in individual foreign markets and in the wider global environment is the hallmark of modern global strategy. Bartlett and Ghoshal[54] describe the integrated global firm as "transnational", but they offer this same focus on integrating capability-leveraging activities across subsidiaries and developing capabilities at managing the integrated global organization. In the transnational model, globalization leads to integrating strategic demands for worldwide efficiency, local market responsiveness, and the spread of world-class technology across all national markets. The transnational model also addresses the need for an organizational structure that is capable of controlling this integration without losing the unique qualities of the individual firm. From a structural perspective, the Heterarchical Multinational of Hedlund[55] and the Differentiated Network of Nohria and Ghoshal[56] both find that advantage comes to the global firm that is able to decentralize operational responsibilities to differentiated subsidiaries while supporting strong integration among all affiliates. These scholars have moved significantly away from industry as the determinant of multinational strategy and identified internal processes as critical to the development of transnational (global) advantage in many industries. We can see an evolution of thinking about multinational firms from an industry-driven set of similar organizations to a resource- or competence-type model in which unique heritage and idiosyncratic capabilities are reflected in firms facing similar market demands but meeting these with individual responses toward globalization.

Key Points in the Chapter

1 Geographical dispersion can enhance the ability of physical, human, and organizational resources to provide advantage to MNCs.
2 Complementary and co-specialized assets are often essential to allowing firms to exploit the potential inherent to their firm-specific strategic resources and capabilities.

3 The FSRCs of multinational firms are often related to their original home market conditions. MNCs can also derive new FSRCs
from their multiple international subsidiary operations.

4 The key dimensions of resource strategies are resource-building
and resource exploitation. Both can be enhanced by internationalization, or geographical spread, and globalization, or cross-
market integration.

5 Internationalization offers more markets in which to exploit existing FSRCs and also multiple contexts in which to identify and
develop new FSRCs.

6 Globalization offers economies of scale and scope to support
resource exploitation strategies and organizational learning opportunities to build corporate capabilities for managing complex
operations.

Notes

1 Barney, J.B. (1991) "Firm resources and sustained competitive advantage", *Journal of Management*, 17: 99–120.

2 Tallman, S. and Fladmoe-Lindquist, K. (2002) "Internationalization, globalization, and resource-based strategy", *California Management Review*, 45(1), Fall: 116–135.

3 Nelson, R.R. and Winter, S.G. (1982) *An Evolutionary Theory of Economic Change*. Cambridge, MA: Belknap Press of Harvard University Press.

4 Tallman, S. (2003) "Dynamic capabilities", in D.O. Faulkner and A. Campbell (eds), *The Oxford Handbook of Strategy*, Vol. 1: 372–403. Oxford: Oxford University Press.

5 Teece, D., Pisano, G., and Shuen, A. (1997) "Dynamic capabilities and strategic management", *Strategic Management Journal*, 18: 509–533.

6 Teece, D.J. (1987) "Profiting from technological innovation". In D.J. Teece (ed.), *The competitive challenge: strategies for industrial innovation and renewal*. Cambridge: Ballinger.

7 Dunning, J.H. (1988) "The Eclectic Paradigm of International Production: A Restatement", *Journal of International Business Studies*, 19(1): 1–32.

8 Porter, M.E. (1990) *The Competitive Advantage of Nations*. New York: The Free Press.

9 Rugman, A.M. (1981) *Inside the Multinationals: The Economics of Internal Markets*. New York: Columbia University Press. (Reissued by Palgrave Macmillan, 2006).

10 Porter, M.E. (1998) "Clusters and the new economics of competition", *Harvard Business Review*, November–December: 77–90.

11 Scott, A.J. (2001) *Global City Regions: Trends, Theory, Policy.* Oxford: Oxford University Press.

12 Shaver, J.M. and Flyer, F. (2002) "Agglomeration economies, firm heterogeneity and foreign direct investment in the U.S.", *Strategic Management Journal*, 21: 1175–1184.

13 Pouder, R. and St John, C.H. (1996) "Hot spots and blind spots: geographical clusters of firms and innovation", *Academy of Management Review*, 21: 1192–1225.

14 Much of the following section is derived from Tallman, S. and Fladmoe-Lindquist, K. (2002), n. 2 above.

15 Rumelt, R.P. (1991) "How much does industry matter?" *Strategic Management Journal*, 3: 167–186.

16 Collis, D.J. (1991) "A resource-based analysis of global competition: the case of the bearings industry", *Strategic Management Journal*, 12 (SI): 49–68.

17 Kogut, B. (1997). "The evolutionary theory of the multinational corporation: Within and across country options". In B. Toyne and D. Nigh (eds), *International Business: An Emerging Vision*, 470–488. Columbia, SC: University of South Carolina Press.

18 Hedlund, G. and Ridderstrale, J. (1993) "Toward the N-form corporation: exploitation and creation in the MNC". Institute of International Business, Stockholm School of Economics RP 92/15.

19 Kogut, B. (1985) "Designing global strategies: profiting from operational flexibility", *Sloan Management Review*, 27(1): 27–38.

20 Cantwell, J. and Piscitello, L. (1997) "Accumulating technological competence- its changing impact on corporate diversification and internationalization", Department of Economics Discussion Papers in International Investment and Management, University of Reading, UK.

21 Collis, D.J. (1991) n. 16 above.

22 Kogut, B. and Zander, U. (1993) "Knowledge of the firm and the evolutionary theory of the multinational corporation", *Journal of International Business Studies*, 24: 637.

23 Porter, M.E. (1998) n. 10 above.

24 March, J.G. (1991) "Exploration and exploitation in organizational learning", *Organization Science*, 2(1): 71–87.

25 Rugman, A.M. and Verbeke, A. (2004) "A perspective on regional and global strategies of multinational enterprises", *Journal of International Business Studies*, 35(1): 3–18.

26 Tallman, S. and Li, J.T. (1996) "Effects of international diversity and product diversity on the performance of multinational firms", *Academy of Management Journal*, 39: 179–196.

27 Teece, D.J. (1986) "Transaction cost economics and the multinational enterprise: an assessment", *Journal of Economic Behavior and Organization*, 7: 21–45.

28 Buckley, P.J. and Casson, M. (1976) *The Future of the Multinational Enterprise.* London: MacMillan.

29 Grant, R.M., Jammine, A.P., and Thomas, H. (1988) "Diversity, diversification, and profitability among British manufacturing companies, 1972–84", *Academy of Management Journal*, 31: 771–801

30 Geringer, J.M., Beamish, P.W., and daCosta, R.C. 1988. 'Diversification strategy and internationalization: implications for MNE performance', *Strategic Management Journal*, 10: 109–119.

31 Tallman and Li (1996) n. 26 above.

32 Michel, A. and Shaked, I. (1986) "Multinational corporations vs. domestic corporations: financial performance and characteristics", *Journal of International Business Studies*, 16: 89–106.

33 Cosset, J.C. and Nguyen, T.H. (1991) "The measurement of the degree of foreign involvement", University of South Carolina CIBER Working Paper Series, D-91-01.

34 Delios, A. and Beamish, P.W. (2004) "Joint venture performance revisited: Japanese foreign subsidiaries worldwide", *Management International Review*, 44: 69–91.

35 Geringer, J.M., Tallman, S., and Olsen, D. (2000) "Product and International Diversification Among Japanese Multinational Firms", *Strategic Management Journal*, 21(1): 51–80.

36 Fladmoe-Lindquist, K. and Tallman, S. (1994) "Resource-based strategy and competitive advantage among multinationals", In Shrivastava, Huff, and Dutton, (eds), *Advances in Strategic*

Management, 10a. Greenwich, CT: JAI Press.

37 Kogut, B. (1985) n. 19 above.

38 Hamel, G. and Prahalad, C.K. (1985) "Do you really have a global strategy?" *Harvard Business Review*, July–August: 139–148.

39 Hitt, M., Hoskisson, R., and Kim, H. (1997). "International diversification: Effects on innovation and firm performance in product-diversified firms", *Academy of Management Journal*, 40: 767–798.

40 Johansson, J.K. and Yip, G.S. (1994) "Exploiting globalization potential: US and Japanese strategies", *Strategic Management Journal*, 15: 579–601.

41 Tallman, S. and Fladmoe-Lindquist, K. (2002) n. 2 above.

42 Porter, M.E. (1990) n. 8 above.

43 Nohria, N. and Ghoshal, S. (1997) *The Differentiated Network*. San Francisco: Jossey-Bass.

44 Hedlund, G. (1986) "The hypermodern MNC – a heterarchy?" *Human Resource Management*, 25: 9–35.

45 Hedlund, G. and Ridderstrale, J. (1993) n. 18 above.

46 Porter, M.E. (1990) n. 8 above.

47 Nohria, N. and Ghoshal, S. (1997) *The Differentiated Network*. San Francisco: Jossey-Bass, 208.

48 Bartlett, C.A. and Ghoshal, S. (1989) *Managing Across Borders: The Transnational Solution*. Boston: Harvard Business School Press.

49 Johansson, J.K. and Vahlne, J.E. (1977) "The internationalization

process of the firm: a model of knowledge development and increasing foreign market commitments", *Journal of International Business Studies*, 8 (Spring/Summer): 23–32.

50 Kogut, B. and Zander, U. (1993) n. 22 above.

51 Collis, D.J. (1991) n. 16 above.

52 Bartlett, C.A. and Ghoshal, S. (1989) n. 47 above.

53 Nohria, N. and Ghoshal, S. (1997) n. 46 above.

54 Bartlett, C.A. and Ghoshal, S. (1989) n. 47 above.

55 Hedlund, G. (1986) n. 44 above.

56 Nohria, N. and Ghoshal, S. (1997) n. 46 above.

CHAPTER 6
Integrating Global Strategy

Strategy in Action

"Accenture is a global management consulting, technology services and outsourcing company."[1] That about covers the field for the post-industrial, information age, de-centralized, de-integrated modern economy – in which Accenture is one of the critical major global players. Originally the consulting arm of Arthur Andersen and set up as Andersen Consulting in 1989, Accenture took its current name in 2000 after a nasty split with Arthur Andersen.[2] Registered in Bermuda, Accenture has 180 000 employees in 52 countries serving clients in more than 120 countries, and earned more than $ 23 billion for FY 2008. Yet this only hints at the international involvement of this company and other global professional service firms. Accenture offers a wide range of business services to include consulting, technology outsourcing, business process outsourcing, and customer relations management to a wide variety of industries, from aerospace and defense, to communications technology, to health sciences, to natural resources, to transportation.

Accenture maintains a long list of clients in the United States, but offshores much of their work for these clients to South and Southeast Asia – it reportedly has had more employees in India than the United States since October 2007.[3] Accenture offers extensive business process outsourcing services, allowing client firms and government organizations to move noncore activities to an expert that operates on a more efficient scale – and can use offshore locations if necessary to further improve service and reduce costs.

Accenture also offers ICT management and development services, customer relationship management, supply chain management, and many other consulting and management services, on a worldwide basis and supported by a global knowledge network.

An example is a CRM application for Ireland's Office of the Revenue Commissioners. Revenue officials recognized the potential of Accenture's Knowledge Development Tool on a visit to the Accenture Technology Labs in Sophia Antipolis, France. This application, sourced from an American company, offered database trawling plus security and data access, aggregation, and transformation with provisions for third party Internet searches. Branded by Revenue as their "Profiler", this application assists auditors and offers enhanced understanding of revenue cases. Accenture used the original proprietary proof of concept for Profiler to develop a more generally applicable database analysis tool they call "Case Crawler", which can be customized to a variety of client needs. Accenture's technology labs are located in Chicago and Palo Alto, California as well as France. Thus we see the company bringing resources from a variety of international locations, from inside and outside the firm, together with a government entity in Ireland to both provide a successful service to the client and to expand the company's knowledge base.[4]

Accenture, like many other business and professional service companies, specializes in providing one-time or noncore services to clients from around the world. A great strength for Accenture and other large, multinational, service firms is that they can access knowledge from many locations, whether internal to the company, or available from other suppliers which have been discovered by one of their far-flung affiliates. Does this make these companies guilty of moving jobs offshore from high to low cost locations? In the simplest analysis, yes. However, even as Accenture provides American clients with relatively simple, cost focused services such as call centers from India, this global consulting firm also brings business to highly paid American knowledge workers in their own laboratories and in Accenture's own external supplier network.

Making Strategy

Once international strategic managers have established their goals and objectives, analyzed the business environment and industry competitive situation, and assessed the assets and capabilities available within the firm, they are ready to begin to develop a strategy or strategies for the multinational firm. This step in the strategy process is in some ways a greater challenge than the preceding process. Previously, we were concerned primarily with analysis – what we wanted to accomplish, what the situation was internally and externally, whether we were staying true to the mission of the firm. Now, though, managers need to break out of the analytic, "just the facts" mode of thinking and engage in creative thinking. They need to consider all alternatives, but they also need to recognize (based on the previous analysis) viable alternatives. They need to consider the context: What does their firm need to do *now*, under the current situation, but also consider the impact: Where will this leave the firm in the future, when things might change? They need to be concrete – after all, this is a real firm trying to accomplish a real mission with real resources and constraints, but they need also to be conceptual – there is a wide range of possible alternative courses of action that others have tried and others described, each with its predictable (and unpredictable) outcomes. And out of all this "grounded blue sky thinking", the strategic manager must finally choose a course of action – choose one strategy and let the others go, at least for now. And then they must figure out how to execute the chosen alternative, but that is for the next chapters.

The last chapter focused on the idea that firms are bundles of resources and capabilities, that these can be applied internationally through a combination of resource leveraging (exploitative) strategies and resource-building (exploratory) strategies, together with strategies of increasing international scope and cross-border integration. Discussing these concepts in separate chapters implied a separability of assets and strategy that is not realistic, so the last chapter was about both resources and capabilities and strategies for finding and using them. This chapter focuses on other approaches to strategy in multinational firms; models that are tied to the marketplace rather than the firm's asset base, focused on the technological advantage of the firm, on the role of management in making strategy, and on other aspects of strategic management that complement the resource focus of the previous chapter. Figure 6.1 suggests a key concern about global strategies from a resource-based perspective – that of fit. First, we see the need for internal fit among the FS-RCs, strategy, and governance structures of the firm. If these are not

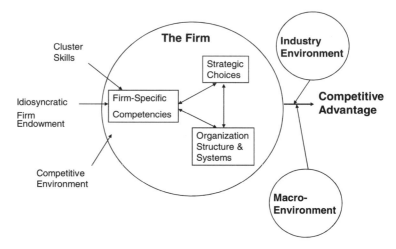

Figure 6.1   Capabilities, configuration, and advantage.

aligned, resources will be wasted, strategies unfulfilled, and governance ineffective and inefficient. Second, we see that the internally generated activities of the firm (and its network of affiliated firms) must also fit with its environment, specifically the industry environment of suppliers, customers, and competitors, and the macro or global business environment of politics, regulation, borders, technology, and other factors outside the control of the firm.

This chapter focuses on the alternatives available to managers at this phase of the strategy process, keeping in mind at all times that real situations have a way of confounding the apparent clarity of conceptual models. For now, though, we can consider what alternatives might be available and what conditions might make each more or less preferred so that we understand how the models match up with reality. One common approach to strategic alternatives proposes that companies may choose to expand into new markets, new product lines, or both – or neither, but rather focus on developing their existing product/market niches. Multinational strategy, of course, is largely about multimarket strategies, but multinational firms are also likely to be multiproduct firms. They must decide how diversified, both across product lines and national and regional markets, they want to be in order to exploit their assets and capabilities to the maximum and gain some financial stability and market power, all while keeping their costs and managerial capability constraints under control. International expansion involves matching products to markets, a frequently evolutionary process. As we have seen, international expansion can also be about the search for assets and capabilities – whether in tandem with market extension or separately. And as we have also seen, as multinational firms expand, they must consider how far to extend themselves and also how much to integrate their international operations – how global to become. Finally, multinational firms also are (or should be!) constantly looking to the future and considering how current strategies can set them up for the future.

The means of expansion also is a frequent research topic in international strategy. Multinational firms can enter markets through market means using *trade* or *licensing* or they can *invest* in production, marketing, sales, or the entire value chain. If investing, they can use *greenfield* startups, committing to building their operations from scratch, or they can *acquire* an existing company or part of a company, or they can set up an *alliance or joint venture* with a local firm or other multinational. Companies must also decide on ownership and control, considering the possibilities of *whole ownership* versus *equity joint ventures, contractual alliances,* or *market transactions*. Once affiliate or subsidiary operations are organized, the MNC must develop policies for the relative roles of headquarters and local subsidiaries, the roles of subsidiaries, and the relationships among subsidiaries. These issues will be dealt with in the next chapter.

Strategies of Fit and the Industry Context

In Chapter 4, we encountered Doz and Prahalad's Global Integration/ National Responsiveness model for international industry analysis,[5] as well as the complementary Configuration/Coordination model from Michael Porter,[6] and the Transnational model of Barlett and Ghoshal.[7] From the view of industrial organization economics or business policy, competitive advantage arises from matching the strategic position of the firm to the competitive landscape of the industry. Understanding this match – or deciding to move in another direction from the industry – is essential to strategic success.

Besides the models mentioned above, George Yip provides a set of mechanisms, or *drivers*, of globalization (and others that pull strategies toward a more national bent) that suggest how multinational firms might determine whether they need to pursue integration or responsiveness and how they reach the strategic postures that these other models describe.[8]

Global integration vs. national responsiveness

We will look first at the match of strategy and situation. Not only do industries tend to reward certain combinations of global integration and national responsiveness, but firms can select the degree to which they pursue each of these generic strategies, as well as how much they want to focus on technological sharing or international knowledge exchange as a source of advantage. One of the first and most influential approaches to international strategy was developed from the Industrial Organization model that dominated early business policy studies. The IO model tied success in business to industry characteristics through what has been called the Structure–Conduct–Performance model. This approach proposes that the objective of strategy (or *conduct*) should be to match the firm's position in the market to the characteristics of the industry's structure in order to maximize performance. Any industry or industry segment could be located on a GI-NR diagram, and the strategies of individual firms within any industry could likewise be charted. As described in Chapter 4, the relative importance of global integration and national responsiveness for any industry or industry segment can be estimated, and the strategies of individual firms within any industry can be chosen similarly. In this model, performance success derives directly from positioning the firm correctly on the GI and NR dimensions, to include possibly having to satisfy high demands for both (or for both plus international learning in the transnational model) imperatives. In this model, performance success derived directly from positioning the firm correctly on the GI and NR dimensions, to include possibly having to satisfy high demands for both (or all three in the transnational model) imperatives.

Yip[9] says that global strategy requires a firm to be ready to go anywhere to meet the demands of the market. He describes various drivers of globalization, to include Market Drivers, such as converging customer tastes, global customers and channels, and transferable marketing skills; Cost Drivers, to include global scale economies, experience curve effects, sourcing efficiencies, high product development costs, and rapidly changing technologies; Government Drivers, like lower trade barriers and common standards; and finally Competitive Drivers, such as relatively high levels of trade, global competitors from various countries and continents, and transferable advantage from FSRCs. Firms faced with a strong combination of these drivers will be forced to consider extending their international reach and integrating across markets. Only by adapting strategies (and organizational structures) that are compatible with these environmental pressures, can firms expect to succeed.

The essence of global integration is that operations in many countries are tied together to lower costs. In the simplest version, everything is produced in the home market and exported. However, this "simple global" strategy typically gives way to a more complex situation as firms expand abroad. By breaking down their value-added chains and defining individual activities and their economic drivers, multinational firms are able to site each activity where it will be most efficient. Thus, basic research may be sited in the US or Western Europe where ties to universities are strong, component production may take place in Taiwan, final assembly in China, Latin America or Eastern Europe, and sales and distribution in each local market. By locating world-scale operations in efficient and effective locations, globally integrated multinationals can tap multiple sources of cost saving. In addition, Bruce Kogut (1985) tells us that such firms can arbitrage by switching production between locations depending on issues such as labor unrest, rising exchange rates, or local demand.[10] As these firms spread across many locations, each a market and a specialized production site for the worldwide system, they may also see opportunities for local adaptation in marketing, sales, distribution, and service, but possibly also in final assembly and surface design – moving to a strategy combining the two generic imperatives. Equally, firms in consumer industries that begin as highly internationalized, but not integrated, multinational networks, may well start moving activities that are subject to strong economies of scale to regional or global centers, a strategy that has become ever more viable as computer-controlled manufacture has led to mass customization in ever more industries.

This model suggests that strategists in multinational firms must focus on industry and competitive structures in the analytic phase and on properly positioning the firm to most accurately reflect the demands of the industry in choosing a corporate strategy. In some industries, consolidation of operations and integration of markets would offer the greatest benefits, while others would call for operations to be dispersed across national markets and managed largely independently. Bartlett and Ghoshal[11] likewise consider that the specific demands of customers in different industries will tend to drive companies toward strategies weighted more along one dimension than the other two – cosmetics toward responsiveness, basic manufacturing toward integration, and technology-intensive industries toward international learning. However, they also introduced other key ideas into the mainstream strategy debate that began to move multinational strategy out of its focus on industry.

These ideas included the possibility that subsidiary or affiliated companies might play differentiated strategic roles within the larger multinational firm. They also suggested that strategic success might derive from the motivation of the people in the firm translated through a more flexible structure and control systems focused on soft, culture-based means rather than strong central control and formal reporting systems. While clearly derived from integration–responsiveness theory, the Transnational Firm concept treats companies as assemblies of people with choices and preferences rather than as somewhat mechanical corporate actors. The need to match internal controls to strategic preferences, to structure according to internal needs, to manage people as important individuals and subsidiaries as independent, but inter-related, parts of a corporate network are all emphasized within this model, opening the way for consideration of other strategic considerations.

Despite this, strategic options in the transnational framework were ultimately limited by industry characteristics. Firms in a consumer-oriented industry that focus on cost-efficient global production of a single product have been and will be strategic losers, no matter how well their strategy, corporate structure, and reporting and control systems are integrated. The strategic manager must understand industry drivers, but must also understand that strategy is as much a product of structural constraints and individual perception as it is of grand mandates – the "administrative heritage" of the firm limits the usefulness of some strategies while greatly enhancing others, and managers need to know the difference. This insight combined with developments in strategic management to lead to the next major framework for multinational strategy.

Markets, alliances, and hierarchies – how best to access markets

During the time that industrial organization economics was being developed into a model of international markets and strategies, a second approach to the multinational firm rose from another economic perspective. In 1976, Peter Buckley and Mark Casson applied Ronald Coase's transactions cost economics[12] to analyzing the decisions of firms in the international marketplace.[13] Their "internalization model" provided a rationale for the existence of multinational firms by suggesting a rigorous analytical approach to the decision to undertake foreign direct investment. Internalization theory posits that firms will choose the lowest cost site for each activity and will use market means to fulfill market demands through exports from the home market or licensing to local firms, up to the point where market governance becomes more costly than internalizing controls. They say that high market transaction costs are most likely in vertically integrated process industries, knowledge-intensive industries, quality-intensive industries, and communication-intensive industries.[14] In such industries, the risks that cross-border markets will go awry are high, and firms are most likely to internalize these markets by foreign direct investment. Thus, companies selling tropical fruits are likely to want control over production, storage, shipping, and distribution in order to control quality, while professional service firms are likely to establish wholly-owned offices in foreign cities in order to ensure that their knowledge and skills are transmitted accurately to clients.

An interesting aspect of internalization theory[15] is that the theory works at the level of the individual economic transaction – the basic exchange of a good or service for an agreed compensation. However, because individual transactions are difficult to track and decipher, the theory is applied by classifying all transactions in an industry by their potential transactional costs – the costs of shipping, but also of identifying transaction partners, bargaining, monitoring, and punishing improper behavior. Thus, if information technology is seen as involving risky transactions because of the ease of misapplying knowledge and the difficulty of identifying culprits before they cause significant damage, then firms in this industry in general will be expected to establish equity positions, either joint ventures or wholly-owned subsidiaries, in foreign markets. This model has considerable power in identifying in which industries firms pursuing market-seeking (Chapter 1) strategies will prefer to use exports, licensing, or foreign direct investment. Conceptually, it offers tools for individual firms engaged in specific transactions in specific markets to analyze their positions, but it has proven to have limited practical value for the purpose, or for explaining when and how multinational firms might want to pursue resource-seeking strategies through foreign investment – though, again, it can theoretically be applied to determine how to execute such decisions as well. The problem is that each firm has unique assets – those FSRCs again – which might or might not require the protection of ownership, and which might or might not be at risk in a particular market, Russia for instance, but not in another – perhaps France.

Economic power models and economic efficiency models purport to have little in common – one is all about using trade and investment to distort markets in order to access monopoly profits, while the other focuses on establishing the most efficient transaction governance so that the firm can gain advantage even when faced with an efficient market. Both, however, look primarily at industry and market conditions to extract rules appropriate to the majority or preponderance of firms in a population, but are not oriented toward identifying why a specific firm might be better off in a specific strategy. They don't do well when asked why Renault is participating in the Japanese market via a joint venture with Nissan, while BMW sells cars made in Germany to consumers in Japan through a dealer network, but sells at least some of its vehicles in the US from a factory in South Carolina. These considerations require a much more detailed look at the firm and its strategy.

Strategies of Fit to the Capabilities of the Firm

The last chapter discussed the possibilities of exploiting existing resources and capabilities and also of seeking new assets in foreign markets and through processes of internationalization and globalization. Simply possessing or accessing unique resources and capabilities is insufficient to ensure competitive advantage – these FSRCs must be applied in a way that supports their characteristics and appeals to the market. A great technology applied to a delicate, unreliable piece of equipment may have a very limited audience, and a great solution to a problem not relevant or meaningful to any potential customer base can easily die on the vine – a common disappointment to many an entrepreneur. Market power and industrial organization-based strategic considerations push the firm to match the structure of the industry, and transaction-cost economic or internalization models encourage firms to seek efficiency within the parameters of the industry. Resource-based thought suggests that strategies need to reflect the resources and capabilities of the firm in addressing markets and in organizing to the task. We have developed these ideas at length in the previous chapter, but just what strategic decisions and directions will properly use internationalization and globalization to exploit existing and build new FSRCs – and how do these ideas fit with earlier models?

Asset-seeking investments are not just aimed at strategic, rent-yielding assets but at complementary or even generic assets. Multinational firms have long sought foreign locations for manufacturing, but offshoring strategies have become more popular in recent years for large – and even not-so-large – firms from most industrial countries. Low wages, skilled and motivated workers in many emerging economies, improved communication and transportation, all make participation in the most productive locations around the world more rewarding. As more firms become experienced at foreign production, they have developed capabilities for coordinating dispersed activities, applying firm-specific knowledge resources at a distance, and managing complex logistics, as well as dealing with political and regulatory concerns in many nations. Of course, on the other side of the production process, firms have likewise become experienced and skilled at understanding local markets, adapting products, managing regulatory concerns, and using local partners and representatives to better access foreign markets, both in combination with local production and as part of a worldwide network of production facilities. The key is that multinational firms are becoming ever more skilled at efficiently matching upstream productivity with differentiation in downstream value-added activities.

At the same time, managers must understand what *their* company can do and what it does well. Not every company has the managerial skills or depth to manage effectively an international network of facilities and markets. Some may look to outsource production to foreign suppliers but keep their own focus close to their home markets, while others find that they need close control of production but can use exports to access markets around the world. Applying existing capabilities in new markets is not easy – the concept of *liability of foreignness*[16] is based on a common reality – particularly for less experienced firms. Even more so is the case of learning from foreign investment. Foreign partners and competitors are not typically interested in providing new competencies to a multinational that is trying to tap into the local skill set, so the multinational must have a well developed capacity for identifying and internalizing knowledge – and be able to communicate this capacity to its local subsidiary.

As in any resource-based model, firm-level performance does interact with the environment of the firm, particularly the terms of competition in its industry, to drive performance. However, as multinational firms move toward superior processes, better technologies, and more efficient adaptation to local needs, they are driving their industries toward more global competition as much as they are reacting to the demands of the industry. In a world of information technology, multinational firms are finding that conservative, opportunism-avoiding, defensive strategies cannot win in the long term – in any industry. The future appears to be about radically decentralized resources integrated by central coordination, not headquarters control. Manufacturing has perhaps led the way toward the new global strategy, but services are rapidly adopting global market perspectives and strong learning ethics as information technologies provide new efficiencies. Firms still adapt to local environments, but do so within a flexible global strategy that emphasizes corporate-level firm-specific capabilities. Industry characteristics still favor some competencies over others, but competitive advantage is more than ever a matter of unique firm-level skills rather than industry-standard practices.

Pursuing Strategies in the International Marketplace

Besides working with and on their resource and capability bases and considering whether to be more global or more responsive in their approaches to the market, multinational firms must develop organizational competencies and strategic approaches to actually pursuing these strategic objectives.

Acquisition in international expansion

Acquisitions are frequent among multinational firms, with a significant percentage of foreign direct investment accomplished through acquisition. Entering foreign markets by acquiring a local competitor is a way to access immediate understanding of local demand and production as well as perhaps internalizing new products or processes. Acquisitions of local firms can be challenging, as well, but acquisition as an entry strategy will be addressed in the next chapter. Here we consider the value of merging with or acquiring multinational competitors as part of a global corporate strategy.

Acquisition (and mergers, but true mergers seem to be relatively rare, particularly as the United States has limited the possibilities for minimizing tax reductions to shareholders through avoiding capitalizing goodwill in mergers) permits firms to collect, in one transaction, a variety of resources and capabilities that they are lacking, or to quickly expand the scope of application of the acquirer's core competencies. Acquisitions also are frequently used as a means of diversifying a company's products or markets. For the firm with a set of products and capabilities that its management believes can be applied in international markets, acquisitions of firms that are related to it through either vertical or horizontal ties allow the extension of competitive advantage more quickly than through organic expansion. Let us consider each of these possibilities for multinational firms.

For the firm with unique products or designs, acquisition of a similar firm, especially one with strong regional or worldwide marketing, distribution or sales capabilities to complement the acquirer's FSRCs, can offer a quick way to access international markets. Competing firms may offer complementary assets to strengthen "core weaknesses" to the acquiring firm and make its proprietary assets more valuable. The new products or superior product technologies can be applied in the acquired firm's production facilities and local-for-local production can be distributed through the existing operations much more quickly than a multinational can build its own downstream operations internally. The acquired firm's brand names may be retained if they are strong, or replaced with the multinational's identity if that is particularly strong internationally. A horizontal acquisition also takes a potential competitor out of the marketplace.

A vertical acquisition of a supplier or a distributor adds production facilities or distribution facilities to support the core competences of the multinational. Again, by internalizing more of the value chain, the acquirer gains control over complementary assets. It can also improve a weak bargaining position along the value-adding chain of an industry sector if it feels that a supplier or customer is accumulating an excess share of the available consumer surplus. This can lead to unexpected transactions. For instance, until 2006, Lenovo produced personal computers in China under contract to IBM. Ten years earlier, IBM might have considered buying up the Lenovo facility if it felt that the quality of work in China was adequate and productivity high, but that it needed greater control over inventories or perhaps wanted to leverage the facility to enter the local Chinese market on a large scale. Of course, what happened instead was that Lenovo bought the entire IBM personal computer business, including brand name, design, marketing, distribution around the world, and so forth to go with its core competency in making quality personal computers at a low price. IBM felt that their assets and capabilities could no longer generate economic rents in a commodity market, but Lenovo apparently saw IBM's strengths as complementary to its unique manufacturing efficiency – whether this was a good decision is still to be seen, though, as Lenovo has dropped the IBM label in favor of its own. Nestlé built much of its international network of food companies and brands through acquisition, often without changing the name or even most of the locally produced goods. Rather, it brought superior marketing skills, process abilities, financial strengths, and so forth to acquisitions that were smaller, financially weaker, under cost pressures, or in need of some new product ideas.

As many multinational firms are also multiproduct companies, acquisitions can also be used to access new product lines for international markets, not just for local entry. Thus, when Daimler-Benz felt that it needed a mass market capacity to complement its luxury brands, it acquired Chrysler of the US, even though Benz already had a significant presence in the US luxury car market. This gave DaimlerChrysler a much larger production capacity to apply its

engineering innovations, to add volume discounts on parts purchases, and to support its finances with many more loans to many
new customers. Daimler did not have to devalue the Mercedes badge
by moving it down-market, and its engineering skills could improve
the mid-market cars and trucks of Chrysler while amortizing its
technology investments widely. While obviously a related acquisition, Chrysler operated largely in different market segments than
Daimler-Benz and allowed the German firm to take a shot at vastly
expanding its possibilities in the automobile and truck industry. As
it turned out, the entire merger-turned-acquisition was not handled
well, and while some of the expected benefits seem to have accrued
to both sides, the differences in corporate cultures, size and scope,
customer bases, and so forth left the two firms with too little in
common and too many conflicts, and Chrysler was sold off in 2008.

In a somewhat more aggressive approach, multibusiness multinationals also use acquisition to enter entirely new lines of business.
For instance, DuPont used international acquisitions to move into
new product lines such as fibers (Kevlar). For a firm considering
moving into an essentially new industry, acquisition is often the
only realistic option – internal development of businesses requiring
completely new capabilities is unlikely to succeed. Research suggests
that diversifying simultaneously into new business lines and new
markets is risky,[17] but some firms have made a specialty of looking
to foreign sources for new products and capabilities derived from
location-specific characteristics unique to the firm's experience.

In other cases, acquisitions are targeted at the firm-specific competencies of the target firm. Companies with large capacities for
effective manufacturing, for widespread distribution, for intensive
sales, often need high value products to move through their value
streams, and either feel that they are in a weak bargaining position for market transactions or that they need to lock in access to
core products or technologies. For instance, major pharmaceutical
companies often identify biotechnology products that are under development in small, often university-affiliated, firms and acquire the
biotech firm. From the perspective of the larger firm, it can use a
variety of such innovative products to fill out its capacity for conducting trials and gaining regulatory approvals in various jurisdic-
tions and to get the most value from its marketing and distribution
capacity. If the big pharmaceutical firms contracted to sell products,
they would be likely to pay a higher market price (particularly as the

small firm would have to pay for a likely inefficient effort at testing and approval) for the rights to the product and would become very vulnerable to underbidding by other pharma companies. Internalizing such products and technologies secures rights, minimizes the costs to the entire value-adding chain, and eliminates competition for access to unique and valuable properties.

So we see that global strategic objectives can be, and frequently are, pursued through acquisitions of multinational targets, whether competitors, suppliers, or customers. Acquisitions offer the chance to internalize specific, known assets and capabilities, to make strategic moves quickly as compared to internal development, to take competitors out of the marketplace, to rationalize supply and distribution, and to establish a balance of rent-earning and complementary assets. On the other hand, acquisitions can be expensive, can result in unexpected organizational clashes or the loss of key human assets (as in the DaimlerChrysler example), lock in inefficiencies, and create managerial nightmares, particularly for firms with little experience at integrating such assets. When the problems with acquisition seem likely to exceed the potential benefits – and research suggests that this is often the case[18] – but the firm needs access to resources and capabilities that it does not have in hand, an alternative that has become more and more popular is the use of strategic alliances.

Strategic alliances and multinational strategy

As with mergers and acquisitions, alliances of various sorts are commonly used to enter new local markets. The pluses and minuses of this approach are addressed in Chapter 8. Here, we will look at the potential benefits of strategic alliances with other multinational firms, or with local firms for the purpose of supplying international markets. From a resource-based perspective, alliances (to include shared equity ventures, whether partnerships, partial acquisitions, or formal joint ventures) provide access to resources and capabilities without requiring the long-term capital investment of internal development or the upfront costs of an acquisition. In many cases, complementary resources are needed for only a temporary application, and "renting" assets through alliance is more cost effective than "buying" them through acquisition – or "making" them internally, for that matter. There are a variety of possible drivers for the alliance decision, which we address here.

The primary condition that encourages the use of alliances is when a firm considering a new strategic opportunity recognizes that it needs additional resources that will support or complement its own strengths. If such resources are accessible through open markets at a fair price, they may well be bought as needed, but if they are more specialized or limited in availability, free market transactions at a fair price may be impossible. In that case, an acquisition can bring in new assets, as described above, but will also include a variety of unwanted resources, management headaches, and large investments. If the assets cannot be developed internally or purchased directly or indirectly at a reasonable cost, they can often be accessed by contracting with the current owner or through limited equity participation. Alliances and joint ventures provide access to resources without destroying the target firm, indeed, often without even exhausting its supply of the asset in question. Key human resources are not placed under new management or into new organizations (at least not permanently – they may well be seconded to a joint venture for a time), and often do not have to relocate. Upfront investment is limited, particularly if an equity arrangement means that both parent firms can participate in cash flows from the alliance. In this case, only direct costs of personnel and equipment need be borne, and not the costs of discounted future cash flows to the target's shareholders. Incentives remain in place, face is not lost, individuals feel much less pressure to respond negatively than to an acquisition.

A good example of the use of alliance in place of acquisition that is contemporaneous with the Daimler-Benz acquisition of Chrysler is the 1999 Renault-Nissan equity joint venture. Looking for new markets for its expertise in automotive design and manufacturing, wanting to become a player in markets outside its core, but short of capital and with limits to its skills in manufacturing and reputation for reliability, Renault began to look for a relationship with a Japanese carmaker in 1998. Toyota and Honda were both highly profitable at home, in North America, and even in Europe (though faced with obstacles). Nissan, however, while still second in sales among the Japanese to Toyota, was struggling with massive losses over much of the 1990s and with a huge debt burden of over 4 trillion yen (nearly $ 40 billion) and a net loss of 14 billion yen (well over $ 100 million) for FY 1998 on shrinking unit sales.[19] Renault proposed to provide a new chief operating officer, in the person of Carlos Ghosn, to Nissan to dramatically cut its costs and improve its efficiency. Renault would take an equity share in Nissan and the automobile operations of the two firms would be operated as a joint venture. Renault could not afford the investment required to build its brand from the ground up in Asia, much less to rebuild its poor image in North America. It also could not afford to take on the totality of Nissan's debt. However, its CEO, Schweitzer, thought that Ghosn had the skills to rebuild Nissan's operations as he had done for Renault. The joint venture and partial acquisition did not generate the sort of xenophobic popular and governmental response that previous attempted buyouts of major Japanese firms had engendered, freeing Ghosn to wield a heavy ax in cutting Nissan's headcount dramatically, closing plants in Japan, and reducing the number of suppliers by a dramatic proportion. While risky, the ongoing senior Japanese role in Nissan made this strategy successful, even as Nissan's skills in engineering and manufacturing became available to Renault, much to its benefit. Ghosn successfully returned Nissan to profitability, cut its debt load dramatically, and raised its sales and market share in the key North American market. At the same time, Renault has launched successful new models in Europe and is no longer seen as a sick company tied to the French market. Ghosn has recently become the CEO of the joint companies, even as their cross-holdings of equity shares have increased – all as DaimlerChrysler lost billions and then disintegrated in the face of executive bailouts, losses, culture clash, and the like.

The strategic roles of subsidiaries

Most models of the multinational firm developed prior to 1989 treated subsidiaries as essentially undifferentiated units that followed the direction of the central headquarters operating via a corporate structure (which we will discuss in the next chapter) that varied little around the world. Bartlett and Ghoshal's idea of the transnational corporation dramatically changed that perception, though.[20] They specified four formal roles for subsidiary operations and described different strategic roles for each. The *Strategic Leader* is a large and capable subsidiary located in a major market, and is expected to provide strategic direction to the worldwide firm to include other subsidiaries and affiliates in its business line on a regional or worldwide basis. A highly capable national organization in a less important market is seen as a *Contributor*, able both to apply the capabilities of the multinational firm in the local market and to capture the benefits of the local context and add them to the company's worldwide solution set. Less capable subsidiaries in less critical markets are expected to act as *Implementers*, acting at the direction of the headquarters or of a Strategic Leader, primarily as sales and marketing arms and as local-for-local manufacturing. Finally, they describe *Black Holes* – subsidiaries that are located in strategically important markets, but that have very limited capabilities. Multinational firms must focus on developing Black Holes into more competent operations, as sacrificing key markets is seldom a positive strategy. The weakness of typologies as theories is apparent in this case, as the only strategy available to the firm (given that the size of the market is beyond the control of the firm) is to move the Black Hole directly toward a Strategic Leadership role, which seems to be asking a lot of a weak organization. In many cases, subsidiaries in critical markets may be more in the implementing or contributing modes based on their capabilities – and even on the strategic needs of the global company. Dispersed leadership has great possibilities, but also has some serious limitations, and not every subsidiary in a large market may be desired as a leader. However, Bartlett and Ghoshal clearly made their point that different subsidiaries can play different roles in the multinational firm.

The issue of a strong strategic role for select subsidiaries has been the subject of other researchers. Gunnar Hedlund described what he called a "heterarchy" (as opposed to a hierarchy) as an emerging form for Scandinavian multinationals as early as 1986.[21] The multinational heterarchy not only offered strategic leadership of subsidiary businesses to dispersed subsidiaries, but moved normal central headquarters functions such as product and process research and development to key international markets. This sort of model is seen in ABB and other firms from smaller countries where the home country headquarters role is reduced to the point of being the financial center, with considerable travel by top executives and virtually all business line control dispersed to key subsidiaries. Indeed, even when retained in the home market, product line management often seems to end up with plant management rather than administrative leaders.

Even more specific to the issues surrounding strategic roles for subsidiaries is the work of Julian Birkinshaw and various co-authors.[22] Birkinshaw describes how the literature of subsidiary strategic roles has developed from recognizing specialized roles, through recognizing that the roles of any individual subsidiary evolve over time, to seeing subsidiaries as players in networks rather than simple members in a hierarchy. With these changing visions of the subsidiary role has come a recognition that market positioning and resource development must be understood *at the level of the subsidiary itself*, rather than from the headquarters perspective. Birkinshaw also suggests that the national subsidiary, as a quasi-independent company, is disappearing in favor of location-tied activities that report to global activity managers, whether in R&D, marketing, or manufacturing. As a consequence, the local subsidiary has a decreasing strategic role in choosing markets – its activities are likely to be given market direction based on their roles in global supply chains. However, the local units often play key roles in accumulating resources and capabilities, particularly those oriented toward conducting operations as opposed to managing the worldwide organization. Birkinshaw suggests various mechanisms by which multinational firms try to offer a degree of independence to subsidiary managers, while still tying them to the overall organization. Informal organizations such as global account management groups made up of individuals from different locations and positions, task forces, internal markets – all encourage innovation and individualism, but within the system. A key insight from Birkinshaw is that even as markets are becoming more integrated, with less pressure for local adaptation, resource accumulation is becoming more heterogeneous and innovation focused, reversing the old model of centrally held standardized assets being applied to differentiated local markets. The subsidiary is playing a new, but probably more critical strategic role in the modern networked multinational firm.

SUMMARY

This chapter has presented various outlooks on strategy making for multinational firms. It begins with the concept that strategic success is tied to matching the actions or market positioning of the firm to the characteristics of the industry sector in which the firm competes. It then offers an alternative approach that suggests that strategic success is more likely to come from matching the actions of the firm to its resources and capabilities, both in seeking markets and in seeking to augment these very assets. Finally, we look at the use of mergers and acquisitions and alliances as ways to pursue strategic initiatives and at the emerging roles of subsidiary organizations as strategic players in the network multinational firm.

Of course, all of these perspectives are relevant to the issue of creating and pursuing strategies. The firm that identifies a relatively uncontested market niche cannot really expect to shine in that position unless it has the resources and capabilities to offer the right products to the customers forming that niche. On the other hand, many firms have proven to be very good at making things that customers don't want or have lost their taste for, so even the staunchest adherent to resource-based models must be cognizant of the market (or lack of market) for their output. The fit of resources and capabilities (sometimes called core competencies), strategy (behavior), and demand in international markets is a triangular relationship for which every leg must offer some support. Indeed, the next chapter suggests that the firm really must be concerned with an internal triangle of resources, strategy and structure and the fit of this multidimensional offering with the external environment, if truly sustainable competitive advantage is to be gained. We will pursue these ideas in Chapter 7. For now, we must be aware that making strategy involves many considerations, each of which has an effect on all the others.

Further, pursuing these multiple layers of fit often requires inputs from beyond the original boundaries of the firm. In these cases, skills must be brought under the umbrella of the firm, whether through internal development, market purchases, acquisition of the firm which owns the needed assets, or temporary alliance with the original owners in order to access – to rent – the needed assets. The modern firm must develop its skills at identifying as narrowly as possible just what makes it unique and allows it to earn economic rents – and then its skills at outsourcing, offshoring, allying, and otherwise arranging to tap into superior sources of those complementary resources needed to generate the profits that are potentially available in its internal skill set. These may well come into the firm through its subsidiaries and affiliates in foreign markets rather than home-based innovative activities. The stimulation of novel location and competition can often outstrip the application of even vast resources in a familiar setting in the race to have the newest inputs – and outputs.

Key Points in the Chapter

1 Strategy making involves a major shift in focus from analytic, reactive, past-focused thinking to creative, proactive, future-oriented thinking.

2 Strategies of fitting the demands of an industry tend to be mechanistic, requiring strategic managers to understand and match the requirements of their particular business, whether through positioning power or through structural efficiency, and leaving relatively little room for innovation.

3 The classic decision in global strategy-making is that of global integration and local responsiveness. Originally seen as a strict trade-off, newer models suggest that MNCs can seek integration in some activities, usually upstream, and responsiveness to local markets in others, usually downstream.

4 Organizational learning across boundaries, as opposed to simple production efficiency, is becoming an ever-more-critical aspect of global strategy in the post-industrial world.

5 Once a strategic focus is decided, the selection of means of transferring competitive advantage becomes an essential choice – does an MNC use licensing, exports, direct investment, or alliance to enter new markets? Or possibly a mix of all these?

6 Global strategy is about accessing new capabilities and resources as much as exploiting existing ones, making country strategies much more complicated.

7 Acquisition is the most common means of foreign direct investment – it is faster than a startup and does not increase competitive pressure as much, but does require a mix of corporate and national cultures that can create many difficulties.

8 In the fast-moving world of technology, strategic alliances as opposed to acquisitions are becoming more popular. They are less expensive in all ways, faster, and more flexible. New contracting and communication methods have reduced the risk of partnering with an opportunist less risky.

9 Whatever their ownership and management form, individual subsidiaries are taking on much more strategically significant roles in MNCs, often acting as the global headquarters for a worldwide product division as well as a local representative.

Notes

1   http://www.accenture.com/Global/
    About_Accenture/Company_
    Overview/Company-Description.htm.
2   http://en.wikipedia.org/wiki/
    Accenture.
3   http://en.wikipedia.org/wiki/
    Accenture.
4   http://www.accenture.com/Global/
    Consulting/Customer_Relationship_
    Mgmt/Client_Successes/
    GeantStrategy.htm, "Ireland office
    of the revenue commissioners: serv-
    ing a community".
5   Prahalad, C.K. and Doz, Y. (1987)
    *The Multinational Mission: Balanc-
    ing Local Demands and Global Vi-
    sion*. New York: The Free Press.
6   Porter, M.E. (1990) *Competitive
    Strategy: Techniques for Analyzing
    Industries and Competitors*. New
    York: The Free Press.
7   Bartlett, C.A. and Ghoshal, S.
    (1989) *Managing Across Borders:
    the Transnational Solution*. Boston,
    MA: Harvard   Business   School
    Press.
8   Yip, G.S. (2003) *Total Global Strat-
    egy II*. Upper Saddle River, NJ: Pear-
    son Education International.
9   Yip, G.S. (2003) n. 8 above.
10 Kogut, B. (1985) "Designing global
    strategies: profiting from operational
    flexibility", *Sloan Management Re-
    view*, 27(1): 27–38.
11 Bartlett, C.A. and Ghoshal, S. (1989)
    n. 7 above.
12 Coase, R.E. (1937) "The Nature of
    the Firm", *Economica*, 4, 386–405.

13 Buckley, P. and Casson, M. (1976)
    *The Future of the Multinational En-
    terprise*. London: MacMillan.
14 Buckley, P. (1988). The Limits of Ex-
    planation: Testing the Internalization
    Theory of the Multinational Enter-
    prise. *Journal of International Busi-
    ness Studies*, 19(2): 181–194.
15 And   the   close   non-international-
    specific   cousin   of   internalization,
    transaction cost economics – see
    Teece, D.J. (1986) 'Transaction cost
    economics and the multinational en-
    terprise: an assessment', *Journal of
    Economic Behavior and Organiz-
    ation*, 7: 21–45.
16 Liability of Foreignness is the idea
    that entities entering a foreign en-
    vironment will be put at a disadvan-
    tage because of their unfamiliarity
    with cultural and institutional con-
    ditions that result in inefficiencies
    in operations and ineffective inter-
    actions with the foreign local market.
17 Kumar, M.V.S. (2009) "The rela-
    tionship between product and inter-
    national diversification: the effects of
    short-run constraints and endogen-
    eity", *Strategic Management Jour-
    nal*, 30: 99–116.
18 Sirower, M.L. (1997) *The Synergy
    Trap*. New York: The Free Press.
19 "Renault/Nissan: The Making of a
    Global Alliance". In C.A. Bartlett,
    S. Ghoshal, and P. Beamish, (eds),
    Transnational Management, 5th edn,
    pp. 587–610, McGraw-Hill Irwin:
    Boston.

20 Bartlett, C.A. and Ghoshal, S. (1989) n. 7 above.

21 Hedlund, G. (1986) "The hypermodern MNC - a heterarchy?" *Human Resource Management*, 25: 9-35.

22 Birkinshaw, J. (2003) "Strategy and Management in MNE Subsidiaries", in A.M. Rugman and T.L. Brewer (eds), *The Oxford Handbook of International Business*, pp. 381-401. Oxford: Oxford University Press.

CHAPTER 7
Global Strategy, Global Structure

Strategy in Action

There are few industries that are more critical to the modern information economy and more global in scope than the semiconductor sector. There are also few industries with a more complicated structure and more de-integrated value-adding chains across companies. Most of us are familiar with Moore's Law: the number of transistors that can fit on a chip will double every 18 months with the corollary that the price of chips will stay essentially flat, so that the cost per transistor will halve every 18 months. The consequence, particularly lately, is that the cost of chip fabricating facilities to make these ever-more-complex micro circuits doubles at almost the same rate. Fabricating facilities – "fabs" – have gone up in price from $ 14 million in 1966 to some $ 6 billion in 2009, with two new "Giga-Fabs" for TSMC (Taiwan Semiconductor Manufacturing Company).[1] A consequence of this expensive, highly specialized manufacturing is that relatively few of the microprocessor firms that come to mind actually make silicon chips any more. Rather, "silicon foundries", companies that specialize in making, rather than designing, chips own most of the production apparatus in the industry.

Earlier in its history, most chipmakers were vertically integrated designers and manufacturers, and often made even the specialized equipment to make chips. Software, computer-assisted design programming and equipment, photolithography equipment, and so forth have been made by specialist suppliers for decades. As chips became more complex and production more difficult and expensive, though, fewer of the design and marketing firms could fill the capacity of a fabricating facility on their own. Some, such as IBM and Samsung, have teamed up to operate facilities within alliances, others make only highly specialized or innovative chips and outsource the rest, but many have gone "fabless". These firms have either been founded as design and sales operations, created with the intent of using contract manufacturers, or have gone the same route as Advanced Micro Devices. AMD, Intel's only serious competitor, spun off its manufacturing facilities in 2008. This move came in response to its own cash crunch, shrinking markets, and rising costs and resulted in the creation of Globalfoundries, majority owned by investment funds controlled by the government of Abu Dhabi.[2] The result is that the semiconductor value-adding process has been largely de-integrated, with only the largest producers, such as Intel, still making their own product.

Another aspect of the industry that is closely tied to vertical de-integration of design and manufacturing is the role of government. *The Economist* points out that there are 40 fabrication facilities under construction around the world, with 35 in Asia, three in the US, and only two in all of Europe. Much of this shift to Asia is tied to governmental industrial policy.[3] Taiwan, South Korea, and now China are all encouraging companies such as TSMC, Hynix and Samsung of Korea, and Semiconductor Manufacturing International Corporation (SMIC) of China to become world players. Subsidies for construction and production, easy merger and acquisition policies, and market growth are all helping these companies to rapidly take over chipmaking for the world as memory chipmakers such as Qimonda in Germany and the US or Micron of the US, with production in the US and Europe, are struggling to maintain share – or closing in the face of the declining world economy in the case of Qimonda.

This move toward specialization in different value-adding activities is not surprising in the case of semiconductors. For one thing, the products are small and high value, meaning that air freight is commonly used to move chips around. Large quantities of identical products are made at a given time in expensive, ever more technologically advanced plants. While the specific circuits on a chip type are unique and proprietary, the processes for all silicon-based chips are identical, meaning that process secrets and patents have limited value. Every step of the process requires precision and the highest quality standards, but each is very different. The capital intensity, worker skills, process flow, and most other aspects of production vary greatly along the value-adding chain. The competition for sales is global, though differentiated across user industries. We may think of microprocessors and memory chips as parts of our laptop computers, but in reality, many products have chips of various types embedded in them. Global markets, highly specialized steps in production, standardized processes and interfaces, differences in factor intensity from stage to stage, all suggest that the industry and the companies in it will only move toward network organization with time.

Of course, the strategic importance of computing components and the role of government in setting up and supporting the massive and expensive foundries have led to concerns on the part of governments in the industrial world. If US and European firms stop making chips, will they eventually lose their underlying skills? In a crisis, can a hostile force cut off access to needed new chips by isolating East Asia? What if China and Taiwan's ongoing political differences lead to a blockade or even a war? How do we power our toys, cars, planes, machines?

Strategy in such industries must take all of these issues into account. This is a politically and technologically sensitive industry. It is also an industry with strong technological and economic forces that drive efficiency in only a few directions. Brand identity and scale advantages are driving consolidation. With so many external pressures, strategists may feel constrained to follow the industry leaders, but in a world of small and shrinking margins, this too can be risky. Knowing just what your company's core competency is and organizing to isolate it from competition or compromise, while minimizing the cost of other activities (which are being carried out by equally stressed and competitive firms with only slightly different skills), requires skill, attention, and luck, and an ability to see and organize for a world that is going to look quite different tomorrow – and that means tomorrow in terms of the next day and week, not some rhetorical construct for the future.

Strategies are relatively easy to create and much more difficult to execute – including the case of the complex strategies of multinational, multi-product firms. Organizations must be structured; people assigned; systems for control, coordination, reward and punishment established; property, plant, and equipment purchased; supply chains put in place; and a myriad of other tasks accomplished –

over and over again. And to add to the complexity of management, emergent strategies must be encouraged and the entire organization readapted to them. No wonder strategy consultants have long enjoyed their work!

This chapter will first consider how corporate structure and control systems support strategies in the Global Integration/National Responsiveness and Transnational models that have been discussed. Global strategies without global structures are unlikely to be successful – indeed, Bartlett and Ghoshal find that strategy largely develops out of systems and structures that have changed gradually in response to only vaguely recognized imperatives.[4] We will then look at the main model of multinational firm structures other than the integration-responsiveness approach – the Internalization Model. From there, we can consider the idea of the MNE as a matrix or network and the importance of alliances to managing highly diversified, marginally controlled organizations. We will also consider how the demands of the information society are forcing large companies in general to decentralize their structures, change command and control for coordination and communication, and actively seek to bring knowledge into the MNC rather than focus solely on moving it out of the center.

Strategies and Structures – Building the Transnational

Strategic success requires fit with the environment, both macro and industry-level, of the MNC, as we have seen. Even those who do not accept the idea that industry is the *sole* key to superior firm performance understand that a strategy that is out of step with the external environment is unlikely to succeed. Likewise, a strategy that is not supported by a suitable organization is likely to fail. Alfred Chandler launched what is called the Strategy–Structure–Performance paradigm.[5] His research, supported by various more recent studies, among them that of Richard Rumelt, showed that strategy (in his case, the degree of diversification of the corporation) must be followed by structure (in his case, the use of multi-divisional structures to support diversified strategies) in order to generate superior performance.[6]

This imperative has only been reinforced by subsequent models. More recent approaches, such as contingency theory drop the sequential "structure follows strategy" approach of Chandler's pioneering concept, but only in favor of an even more intensely integrated relationship. Strategy is influenced by existing structure, and both must be suited to contextual conditions, but all in a complex, interconnected, adaptive system that can only be seen properly from an overall perspective – partial analysis leads us astray, and only global equilibrium offers long-term success. Beyond this position, evolutionary models of the firm suggest that all the parts of the system in which firms operate are under constant pressure to change and adapt – equilibrium is a convenient part of economic models, but is not likely to be achieved in reality. External forces keep the environment of firms, and MNCs in particular, constantly changing. Firms will evolve to fit new environments either through replacement or adaptation and competition with other firms. Further, as the population of MNCs in an industry evolves, the environment of each firm – which is largely constructed of other firms that also are constantly changing – changes, and the firms must continue to adapt or suffer the consequences. However, firms also adapt their strategic commitments and structural designs as their internal competencies increase. Models that suggest that internationalization is an evolving process suggest that firms tend to enter the international market in tentative steps that gradually become bolder.[7] Likewise, they use structures that begin with minimal commitment of resources and gradually increase in commitment and investment as company management becomes more confident.

MNCs have developed more complex structures as their commitment to the international marketplace has increased. Companies that use only exports and perhaps licensing to sell products abroad may have no more than a small office to handle export sales through agents and royalty payments from licensors. However, as international sales turn into international operations, newly minted MNEs must make some structural adaptations. In an early study, Stopford and Wells connected market strategies to corporate structural solutions.[8] Firms with relatively low levels of international sales and international production tended to use some version of an *international division*. The international division acts as an agent for the product divisions in managing international sales and coordinates international production operations, such as they are. A core of people committed to international activities offers considerable expertise and experience to the market, and can be very effective in operating in many foreign markets with relatively little capital commitment. The weakness of this system is that the rest of the company tends to focus on traditional domestic markets, and the international division has relatively little internal power and influence. As a result, neither problems nor success in the international realm are likely to gain the resources needed either to correct problems or to support success, particularly if product divisions have their own issues at the same time.

Should the firm nevertheless expand internationally, Stopford and Wells see two probable strategic directions and two structural solutions. For the firm with increasing international sales but production abroad of a relatively small number of products, the tendency is toward *area divisions*, or a geographically based organization. Regional headquarters have historically developed out of a country-based, or "mother and daughters", structure, in which separate local operations developed to sell, and eventually make, products that were more or less identical to those produced in the home country. Ford, for instance, before World War II, had operations in many European countries, all making the same Model Ts and Model As and subsequent Ford designs, but all operating largely as independent countries. This organization was largely the result of highly restrictive trade laws in the inter-War years, so that exports from the US were both slow and costly in terms of transport, and subject to high tariffs or small quotas in terms of regulation. Better to set up foreign affiliates and collect dividends. The difficulties of managing widespread operations and the movement toward local product differentiation made for extreme independence, and MNCs responded with regional organizations to provide greater control, and to also coordinate more efficient regional product development, manufacturing, and sales. Procter & Gamble, for instance, originally approached the European market with many independent national subsidiaries, all organized in a similar fashion to P&G in the US – what have been called "mini-parent companies". However, as product technology became more complex and expensive, and as European competitors became stronger, P&G needed a more efficient approach to the region, and set up P&G Europe. This entity began by funding central R&D to create products that individual companies could adopt and adapt, but gradually moved toward regional production of many consumer goods and to regional brand management teams led by brand managers selected from the various Western European country subsidiaries. A focus on customer needs, particularly needs that vary from place to place, within a product category tends to lead to geographically focused organization. Here, internationalization occurs without integration, and organizational structure and control systems develop to support the resulting focus on local differentiation.

On the other hand, Stopford and Wells found that when international sales and production spread across a number of product categories, but at a slower rate, MNCs tended to respond by creating *global product divisions*. This solution essentially takes international responsibility away from the single corporate international division and disperses it to all of the product division managers. This solution is most effective for firms with a variety of very different products, where single country organizations cannot effectively represent all products and the customers for different products are likely to be quite different – a multiproduct multinational strategy such as that of General Electric, for example. Global product divisions offer the opportunity to integrate operations across many countries within each industry sector. For industrial products or consumer products with low cultural impact, such as information technology products, the efficiency gains from regionally or globally scaled R&D, production, and even marketing offset the relatively small benefits of local adaptation – and modern production techniques even allow for levels of mass customization that can adapt, within limits, to local demands. By putting responsibility for international markets on the product divisions, the multinational corporation can avoid the international division situation where international markets receive inadequate support from the product divisions. By organizing around products, technological gains and production efficiencies are emphasized and national preferences subordinated to quality and capability. The global product division emphasizes Ted Levitt's dictum that given globally advanced technology, world-class quality, and globally competitive pricing, customers are more and more willing to forego local preferences for design, taste, or attribution.[9]

Since they focus on corporate strategic and structural solutions, Stopford and Wells did not really look at single product companies, but such firms can be of great importance. In addition, global product divisions within highly diversified firms often act largely as standalone companies with an internal capital market. A third global structure may be the best fit in such a situation – the *global functional structure*. For a company such as Boeing, which sells virtually identical commercial jet aircraft around the world, each value-adding stage is accomplished on a global scale. Production, whether in Tacoma, or for a critical part in Japan or China, happens for the world – 787s will come off one final assembly line for all markets. Procurement, distribution, marketing, and service support all must be controlled by central headquarters as actions in any one location are closely entwined with those in other places. In this sort of situation, organizing the company around business functions or value-adding steps, each with a worldwide scope, can be most efficient.

What about the situation, though, where a company has a wide variety of products offered in many foreign markets, with extensive global or regional production, but a need for local adaptation? Writing in the early 1970s, Stopford and Wells saw that some very multinational firms, with both a high level of overseas sales and a wide array of international products and production, were organized as *product–area matrices*.[10] That is, companies were structured so that one set of executives just below the corporate head were responsible for global product divisions, while another group of equal rank were responsible for area divisions. Unit managers within the matrix reported both to a product line headquarters and to a regional or national headquarters. The need to balance the demands for efficiency and technology that drove success in global products with the demands for local adaptation that drove country-by-country success was expected to lead to a strategic dynamic balance that would keep the firm and its products sharp. However, over time, relatively few firms moved to matrix arrangements. Subordinate managers found that having two bosses led to strategic paralysis rather than dynamism, and internal political struggles were exacerbated. A few firms such as DuPont and ABB had success with matrix organizations, but most that have tried the matrix (including ABB) have reverted to global product divisions, and indeed few companies have attempted formal matrix structures. The difficulty of managing such a complex structure has proven to be greater than the strategic imperative to balance competing market demands.

The structure that seems to have evolved as multi-product multinationals have become more familiar with multiple foreign markets and with managing across boundaries of many sorts is the *global network*. Ghoshal[11] and Nohria and Ghoshal[12] describe this firm in detail, and other scholars have used different terminology to describe the same phenomenon. The network firm describes a condition in which firms may demonstrate various formal structures – most often global product divisions in today's world – but actually operate through a set of informal relationships among the various subsidiaries and affiliates of the firm. Key to the network concept is that the center, the home country headquarters, surrenders its traditional command and control role to focus on fostering communication and coordination among the component parts of the company, while operating decisions are taken at the subsidiary level or between subsidiaries. Another key aspect of the global network, as described by Birkinshaw,[13] is that individual activities in different locations tend to be networked with other similar or related activities, all reporting to global or regional managers, rather than functioning as parts of local hierarchies. Foreign operations structured as formal subordinate companies are disappearing in favor of functionally oriented units located according to principles of comparative advantage and organized in a multinational scheme. We will consider this structure in greater detail later in the chapter.

Markets and Hierarchies

Stopford and Wells considered alternative ways of organizing at the corporate level of the multinational firm, and the work in the integration-responsiveness vein continued to look at how large multinational corporations would structure their administrative functions at the highest levels. Only a few years after Stopford and Wells, though, Peter Buckley and Mark Casson, in their book *The Future of the Multinational Enterprise*,[14] focused structural considerations on the choice of how individual international transactions were governed, differentiating between external market-based transactions and internal transactions governed by managerial decisions. As with Williamson's *Markets and Hierarchies*,[15] published at the same time and also based on the transaction cost economics of Ronald Coase,[16] the Internalization Model proposes that international transactions will be governed through market processes – pricing levels – until the cost of doing so becomes too great, at which point the transaction will be internalized, brought inside the corporation.

Market transactions may be either exports of goods or services or licensing of intellectual property. In the first case, products are made by the multinational in the home market and sold in foreign markets, either directly or by agents. In the latter, a licensee pays fees for using the multinational's intellectual property to then produce locally for the host market. Export transactions must bear the costs of shipping, inventory carrying, market analysis, ongoing bargaining with export agents and distributors, tariffs, and so forth, which may encourage licensing. In both cases, though, governance costs arise when unreliable partners either take advantage of the exporter to extract excess profits or fail to perform as well as expected in marketing, sales, and distribution. In such cases, the transactional costs of external market exchanges can exceed the costs of using internal markets in which both sides of the transaction are part of the same multinational firm and have reduced incentives to cheat one another. Such conditions are particularly likely when the transaction involves information-intensive products or the licensing of complex technologies. In these cases, information asymmetries between seller and buyer make the possibility of improper pricing high, and mean that internal transactions should be particularly effective.

Alan Rugman expands somewhat on the internalization model.[17] He also demonstrates that it is fundamentally compatible with various models from the integration-responsiveness stream. He describes Firm Specific Advantages (FSAs) in knowledge that are tied to the firm, but not to any particular location, and Country Specific Advantages (CSAs) that are tied to specific locations. The key to structuring international transactions is tying FSAs and CSAs together in the most efficient manner possible, whether through external markets or internal transactions. Rugman suggests that the choice between exporting and foreign production rests on a comparison of location-tied production costs in the home and host nations, assuming that the FSAs are the same in either case. If production is preferred in the host country, due to its superior CSAs, then the choice of foreign direct investment or licensing depends on whether internal markets for the knowledge embodied in the FSAs are superior to direct sale of that knowledge. And, while licensing seems inexpensive, Rugman focuses on the risks of dissipating knowledge, the difficulty of determining the correct fee for the license, the difficulty of policing a license, and the difficulty of separating FSAs (which are generally heavy on tacit knowledge) from the originating firm – and concludes that making markets for knowledge is difficult and often fails. Again, knowledge-intensive FSAs are most likely to benefit from internalization, as correct and honest applications from licensees or import agents are more difficult to ensure, requiring internalization and extending the boundaries of the firm to the host country.

The version of internalization theory most closely tied to global strategy, of course, is Dunning's Eclectic Model of the Multinational Enterprise.[18] As described before, this model says that firms will sell in foreign markets if they have ownership advantages (similar to Rugman's FSAs), and will make their products where they sell them if location conditions (similar to Rugman's CSAs) make this more productive. In structuring the governance mechanism for a given transaction, the Eclectic Model suggests that internalization factors, considerations that make internal markets more efficient than external markets (whether for intermediate hard goods or for knowledge), will lead to the extension of firm boundaries, and the creation or enlargement of the multinational firm. As with the other proponents of internationalization theory, Dunning sees knowledge-driven transactions as the most likely to be internalized, particularly when they involve knowledge which is tacit and difficult to codify and transmit indirectly.

Finally, David Teece ties the internalization model of the multinational firm to Williamson's Transaction Cost Economics directly.[19] Williamson's language of the fundamental shift from market to hierarchical governance is obviously applicable to the transition from market to internal governance. Williamson describes bureaucratic internal governance, not internal markets, but with their common heritage in Coasian economics, the two models have obvious connections. Teece shows that Williamson's specification of uncertainty levels, bounded rationality, small numbers bargaining, and transaction-specific investment as opening the transaction to opportunism by either of the partners provides a more detailed and carefully specified analysis of the shift from market to hierarchy, or (in the language of the internalization school) from external to internal governance. In this scheme, the possibility that an exchange partner might be opportunistic, misappropriating rents or resources from the multinational firm, makes the use of market exchange more risky, inducing the multinational firm to buy its potential partner or set up its own operation in the foreign market. When the multinational has few choices of partners, plans to engage in an extended or repetitious set of transactions, and particularly has to make significant investments in order to engage in the transaction(s), the possibility of protecting itself through superior contracting and monitoring becomes more difficult, and it is more likely to internalize the transaction – setting up its own operation or acquiring a putative partner.

Internalization theory tells us a lot about structuring governance for individual transactions, and (depending on the firm's capabilities and the industry's characteristics) can be extrapolated to suggest how much firms will use exports, licensing, or subsidiaries (including joint ventures – we will pick this up next), to enter markets around the world or to control offshore production agreements. In the end, though, internalization models do not say much about how the administrative structure of the multinational firm will be developed to manage these many transactions, whatever their form. We could perhaps guess that primarily export-oriented or licensing firms will be organized in product divisions with small international offices. Firms that have large capital investments in many countries are more likely to create real international headquarters, either on a regional or country basis, or as real global product divisions that consider world markets, not just overseas sales of home production. Still, these models are more complementary than competing – they talk about different things. When Lenovo uses its computer-building skills (FSAs in design, process control, etc.) to make laptops in China (CSAs in labor costs and productivity, a growing home market) and to export them to the United States, we can see the practicality of this. However, when we also consider that Lenovo's corporate headquarters is based in the US and much of its design is done in the US or Taiwan, and its key components come from Intel in California, and so on, it is clear that "structure" is a complex idea and hard to reduce to the export-FDI discussion *or* to the global product vs. regional division argument.

Internalization theory is constructed around the assumption that the MNC is looking at foreign countries in which to market and sell its products or technologies, but the majority of its considerations are equally useful to the choice of in-house or outsourced offshore production. Thus, if a product is such that it can be fully specified, quality control is simple, and opportunistic partners controlled, outsourcing is likely to be preferred. When Nike, for instance, has its sport shoes made by contract manufacturers in China, it is able to monitor the processes and products closely and can quickly and easily discipline a straying supplier. However, when IBM is looking to China as an important site in software development, the need to protect easy-to-pirate software while encouraging complex joint development between Chinese and American (and perhaps other nationalities) programmers suggest that internal management will be more effective and lower risk.

Cooperative Forms – Alliances and Joint Ventures

Multinational firms do not structure themselves around either external or internal markets, nor do they have complete control of all of their subsidiary operations – they often use cooperative strategies to access resources from other firms through alliances, whether contractual agreements or equity participations. Alliance forms bring unique benefits and unique risks and merit consideration on their own, even though they are certainly part of a choice set that runs from exporting through independent agents such as freight forwarders to independently owned foreign firms to complete internalization of the entire value chain from start to finish and in every location.

Andrew Inkpen defines international strategic alliances as (1) being cross-border, (2) created by two or more firms that remain independent, (3) involving ongoing interdependence (not just a one-time affair), and (4) having some uncertainty about the cooperation of the partners (since they *are* independent firms).[20] Alliances run the gamut in increasing level of commitment from training or management agreements through supply or production agreements to franchising to R&D contracts to equity joint ventures and minority acquisitions.[21] These all offer a structural solution for a transaction by which two or more firms can tap into each others' resources and capabilities, but on an as needed, temporary basis. If we consider internal sourcing and the open market as offering a "make–buy" choice for assets, alliances provide what might be seen as the "rent" alternative – key complementary resources are accessed on an ongoing, but not permanent or internalized basis in order to generate superior value-adding processes.

From our resource-based perspective, alliances offer an alternative when a firm does not have required resources and cannot create them internally in a timely and economic manner. If the required resources are not directly available in the marketplace (often the case with tacit capabilities) and an acquisition is problematic, an alliance may well provide the solution. Acquisitions tend to be more expensive than alliances, particularly in up-front costs, they bring in an entire firm's worth of assets, many of which may be irrelevant or even undesirable, they require incorporating a large number of people into the organization, and they often drive off the very individuals from the target firm that are most valuable.

For example, when Toyota decided to consider production in the US, they set up a joint venture (New United Motor Manufacturing International – NUMMI) with General Motors. Toyota had the Toyota Production System and desirable cars in the early 1990s, but did not know if their capabilities would work with US workers (indeed, many at Toyota had serious doubts about American workers). Toyota could have gone ahead with building or buying a plant and hoping for the best, but they were able to access a recently shuttered GM plant in Fremont, California through a joint venture. Not buying the plant reduced their capital investment, and GM could offer expertise in operations other than assembly processes, a distribution network, access to experienced auto workers, and the property, plant, and equipment. These became essentially complementary assets to Toyota's process skills, accessed as GM's capital contribution to the joint venture and paid for by dividends to GM's ownership share and by providing Chevy Novas to GM to sell. Toyota could not buy GM (at least not in 1991), and likely did not want to do so anyway. They could have bought the plant, but the capital investment would have raised the risk in case American workers proved incompetent. The original agreement had an end date, and Toyota seemed to have little fear that GM could actually copy their production system – or, at least, they were very open with their partner. In the end, the JV has continued well beyond its original termination date and continues to build small cars to be sold by both parents.

Strategically, Toyota was able to reduce its risk in producing in and for the US market by keeping their investment low and by having an American partner to deal with unique aspects of the US auto production and distribution system. They accessed GM's dealer network, workers and management, technology, and so forth at low cost. Effectively, they were able to leverage their core competency, low cost production, in a very different environment at low risk and with a solid return on the direct product. More to the point, Toyota learned about using American workers in the TPS and followed up by building its own plants in various locations in North America – but with considerable confidence in their success. In one way, NUMMI was an alliance used as an entry strategy – a topic discussed in the next chapter – but, given the importance of the US market and Toyota's reluctance to move toward foreign production, it also acted as a strategic alliance, a chance to alter the strategic direction of the company by using an equity joint venture structure and cooperative strategy to improve the overall inputs and reduce the risks of failure.

If we look at the drivers of multinational structural decisions, we can see that alliances offer opportunities in all cases.[22] The Toyota–GM example was used to consider the resource and capabilities perspective. Alliances allow firms to bring together sets of resources from the partners that none of the firms could assemble economically alone, and to do so in a relatively fast and inexpensive manner. If we look at the internalization/ transaction cost perspective, alliances offer useful intermediate stages of integration between markets and hierarchies.[23] Contractual alliances offer an exchange of value, but on a complex and typically extended basis. By engaging with a partner for an extended period, the multinational firm can get superior inputs adapted to its particular needs, can get guaranteed supply and avoid sudden cutoffs of inputs, and has an improved set of governance alternatives to simply paying or not buying at the set price (or a negotiated discount) as in a pure market. As commitments grow on both sides, the difficulty of finding an alternative partner grows, transaction-specific investments are made on both sides, greater flexibility may be needed as conditions change over time, and more alignment of economic benefits becomes more important. At this point, equity-based alliances, either direct participations or equity joint ventures, become more common. By investing in the jointly held company, the partners all have a stake in its success and a say in its operation. By taking out their returns in the form of dividends to their equity shares, the partners are encouraged to work together to maximize joint gains. The upshot of all this is a decreased potential for opportunism and consequently lower transaction costs than an exposed market, but hopefully lower bureaucratic costs than if one firm acquired the other – as well as avoidance of the other difficulties of acquisition.

Finally, from the industry fit or strategic behavior perspective that began the chapter, alliances can allow firms to collaborate as they consider where they fit in their industry picture. Thus, a very internationalized firm that wants a local cachet in many markets can ally with local competitors to get a local name and identity – not just to enter single markets, but as a strategic approach to all markets. Such alliances offer local skills, localized downstream value activities such as sales and distribution, political value and they co-opt potential competitors by bringing them together with the multinational. Of course, such collaborationist strategies can be risky, but they are also often very lucrative as they reduce the levels of competition in an industry, both in individual markets and on an international scale.

Global integration requires close cooperation across all stages of the value-adding chain, implying frequent whole ownership. However, with the advent of improved tools for management of ventures, global firms are making greater use of offshore outsourcing contracts in developing countries such as China, India, or Eastern Europe. Though occasional issues such as child labor violations or adulteration of products with harmful chemicals arise, global firms more and more have systems in place to deal with such issues while keeping their global networks together and profitable. Without accumulated experience with managing alliances and joint ventures, the network multinationals described by many scholars, with their need for closely aligned operations by many interdependent suborganizations combined with lowered costs of management and greater flexibility than typically, would be impossible to operate. Neither capital stocks nor executive resources are sufficient to run a differentiated, dispersed network of value-adding activities as a hierarchical structure except in possibly the largest companies. Rather, decentralization of decisions, minimal investment for maximum returns, embeddedness in local communities, and rapid adaptation to a changing environment are all antithetical to tight internal control. The network multinational is becoming more and more a network of alliances and joint ventures.

The Role of the Center and the De-Integration of HQ Activities

If alliances and joint ventures make up most of the cloud of network nodes that characterize operations in the modern multinational firm, how has the role of the center, the corporate headquarters, changed to accommodate their needs? Classic depictions of multinational, multi-business, corporate structures show a corporate headquarters at the top, occupied by the top executives and their staffs, with lines running down and out to a variety of divisional headquarters – whether functional, product, or location-based divisions depending on the issues discussed at the start of the chapter. While in some sense still relevant to formal reporting relationships in many companies, these 'box and wire diagrams' no longer reflect the realities of operational relationships.

Such a picture was perhaps accurate when the primary role of the multinational was to identify products and technologies developed in the home market and move them out, possibly with a bit of repackaging, to foreign markets through exports, licenses, and market-seeking investment. Ideas started at the top and flowed along the lines in the structural diagrams to ever more distant parts (of both the company and the world) until they were sold in some form to a final customer. As we have seen, though, the world has changed, and so have the multinational companies working in it. Ideas are now coming from a variety of places, many unexpected. Manufacturing has been offshored for years, but now business services, both back office and customer focused, are being delivered at a distance by less well paid, but highly competent workers in emerging economies, and even product research and development, once sacrosanct to the central HQ, is conducted in networks of labs scattered around developing Asia, emerging Eastern Europe, and no-longer-isolated Latin America. How does the center maintain control?

Well, perhaps it does not, at least not in the command and control sense understood traditionally. Already in the 1980s, Scandinavian researchers were seeing that multinationals from their small native countries were diffusing their operations around the globe. Swedish firms were well known for moving their manufacturing and downstream activities to larger markets, first in Europe and then in North America and the rest of the world, but the new 'heterarchies' as

Gunnar Hedlund called them were also moving traditional headquarters activities out of the center and out of the country.[24] If Asea
was going to have its largest market and largest manufacturing facilities in Germany, then it made sense to disperse product development
efforts and marketing control to that market, rather than continuing to design products and campaigns for a smaller customer base
in Sweden and hope to appeal to the Germans (or French, British,
Americans, etc.). We have seen this story repeated for many companies from smaller home countries – IKEA, Philips, ABB, Electrolux,
and others. The difference from the traditional area division multinationals of the 1960s and 1970s is that not only do these country
operations design, build, and sell in their local markets, but they design, build, and sell for regional and world markets. *And* they may
well be the world headquarters for major product divisions, to include doing basic research, managing global accounts for marketing,
and controlling further offshore production and distribution. Much
of the work traditionally done at HQ is still done, but no longer in
a central location – the company owned and operated multi-story
headquarters in the capital city of the home country is an expensive
and out of date anachronism.

   An example of this is the decentralization of Asea of Sweden and
later of its successor, ABB, under Percy Barnevik from 1979, when
he took over Asea, until 1996, when he gave up his CEO role to his
designated successor. Barnevik is perhaps best known for organizing and operating a product x area matrix structure for much of
this time. However, an equally dramatic, and possibly more influential, decision was to cut the corporate headquarters to about 10%
of its previous size and responsibility. Let's look at this oft-cited,
but somewhat faded example.[25] Barnevik first set up a large number
of profit centers, each with extended responsibilities, and located
around the world. He then cut the central HQ by 90%, eliminating 30% of the jobs, shifting 30% to the operating companies, and
moving 30% to internal service providers – set up as profit centers.
With the highly internationalized company that resulted from the
Asea–Brown Boveri merger, the many global profit centers were organized into a matrix, reporting to both global business areas and
country organizations. A complex corporation with over 150 000
employees was to be run by a corporate HQ with about 150 executives and staff. The majority of traditionally centralized tasks were
farmed out to the global product divisions (most consisting of a

general manager who was also a profit center and plant manager and a couple of administrative staff) and on to the individual operating companies. Products were developed where they were made and used, not at a lab in Sweden or Switzerland. Marketing plans came from people in direct contact with customers; plants were run by their managers as profit centers rather than cost centers. All in all, a massive organization was managed, not really controlled, by a very small (if very hard working!) group of executives who spent much of their time on the go from site to site.

Hewlett-Packard had a similarly decentralized organization in the mid 1990s. As new products were developed or acquired, they were spun off or set up as new Global Product Divisions, and typically located wherever the base technology originated. Each division was largely responsible for its own value-adding operations and was operated as an individual profit center. Each was part of a worldwide product group, which was responsible for setting up the divisional charters and coordinating marketing, sales, and distribution on a regional basis. Regional managers, such as the president of H-P in Europe, had no control over product development or manufacturing, and had limited input on downstream activities. Their major role was coordinating regional affairs, such as working with the European Commissions, and assisting integration of the divisions based in the region when product coordination was required. This activity was managed, for instance, by creating internal alliances among product divisions, handled through formal contracts, but negotiated through the regional headquarters.

These are but two examples of what is becoming a more common phenomenon – the networked multinational firm that is focused on knowledge collection, transfer, and application – what Yves Doz has called the "Metanational".[26] In this multiproduct multinational, subsidiaries and affiliates are actively involved in prospecting for new knowledge about technologies and products, and the corporation works to collect and combine this knowledge into new capabilities that can then be applied in other markets, even at home – much like the recombination capabilities that Kogut and Zander described and which were discussed above.[27] These models see the multinational firm as an arbitrageur of knowledge, collecting knowhow where it is common and applying it, in combination with related knowledge from other places, where it is unusual and therefore capable of generating rents. The role of the headquarters is much more one of maintaining cooperation and communication among the network of more or less equal, or at least similarly purposed, subsidiaries, affiliates, alliances, contractors, joint ventures, and so forth. Unlike the Transnational Model, which prescribes different roles for different subsidiaries based on market characteristics and rather static capabilities, the knowledge-based multiproduct multinational permits subsidiaries to take varied roles as they have opportunity and capability and to evolve with their markets and with the multinational network itself. Thus, a small central unit can manage – through communication and coordination rather than command and control – a wide-ranging and highly diverse network. The center is a source of guidance more than a command center, which is perhaps the only way that a widespread, diversified, informally organized network firm can function efficiently.

SUMMARY

This chapter began with a description of different types of formal organization used by multinational firms, and developed by scholars concerned with the best fit of the multinational firm to its worldwide industry environment. It then looked at the idea of structuring individual transactions and the impact of transactional characteristics on the relative importance of market versus hierarchical governance structures for individual transactions that are assembled into the firm-level structures described in the first part. We then discussed the idea of alliance structures in more detail, as these are becoming more common and more important to multinational strategy as technology becomes more ubiquitous. Finally, we discussed the changing role of the central headquarters in the knowledge-based multinational. Much less formal, but perhaps even more difficult, than the command and control role in the recent past is the evolving role of the center as context-manager, as webmaster of the network, responsible for setting the terms of internal transaction, but not mandating the content of interactions between profit centers. Keeping market or quasi-market controls in place allows natural coordination to arise rather than using the much more effortful approach of requirement and monitoring of the traditional firm.

Key Points of the Chapter

1 International Divisions are commonly used to manage relatively small-scale, export-based international operations.
2 Companies with large-scale foreign operations but a limited number of product lines tend to organize around regional or area divisions.
3 Companies that make and market a wide range of products internationally tend to favor worldwide product divisions.
4 Complex combinations of global production bases, internationalized innovation, and multinational markets have led to equally complex network organizations that mix wholly- and partially-owned subsidiaries with joint ventures, alliances, and contractual partners for a flexible and reactive organization.
5 The governance of individual transactions is based on relative transaction costs, to include shipping, tariff, bargaining, and opportunism costs.
6 Outsourcing and internal production are complemented by co-operative or alliance transactions, by which the complementary assets of partners are accessed, but not internalized, when neither making nor buying offers the best alternative for accumulating assets.

Notes

1 "Under new management: Briefing on the semiconductor industry", *Economist*, 4/4/09: 71–73.
2 Ibid.
3 Ibid.
4 Bartlett, C.A. and Ghoshal, S. (1989) *Managing Across Borders: The Transnational Solution.* New York: The Free Press.
5 Chandler, A.E. (1962) *Strategy and Structure: Chapters in the History of American Industrial Enterprise.* Cambridge, MA: MIT Press.
6 Rumelt, R.P. (1974) *Strategy, Structure, and Economic Performance.*
Cambridge, MA: Harvard University Press.
7 Johanson, J. and Vahlne, J.-E. (1977) "The internationalization process of the firm: a model of knowledge development and increasing foreign market commitments", *Journal of International Business Studies*, 8 (Spring/Summer): 23–32.
8 Stopford, J. and Wells, L. (1972) *Managing the Multinational Enterprise: Organization of the Firm and Ownership of the Subsidiaries.* New York: Basic Books.

9 Levitt, T. (1983) "The globalization of markets", *Harvard Business Review*, 61: 92–102.
10 Stopford, J. and Wells, L. (1872) n. 8 above.
11 Ghoshal, S. (1987) "Global strategy: an organizing framework", *Strategic Management Journal*, 8: 425–440.
12 Nohria, N. and Ghoshal, S. (1997) *The Differentiated Network*. San Francisco, CA: Jossey-Bass.
13 Birkinshaw, J. (2003) "Strategy and Management in MNE Subsidiaries", in A.M. Rugman and T.L. Brewer (eds), *The Oxford Handbook of International Business*, pp. 381–401. Oxford: Oxford University Press.
14 Buckley, P.J. and Casson, M. (1976) *The Future of the Multinational Enterprise*. Basingstoke and London: Macmillan.
15 Williamson, O.E. (1975) *Markets and Hierarchies*. New York: Free Press.
16 Coase, R.H. (1937) "The Nature of the Firm", *Economica*: 386–405.
17 Rugman, A.M. (1981) *Inside the Multinationals: The Economics of Internal Markets*. London: Croom Helm.
18 Dunning, J.H. (1979) "Explaining Changing Patterns of International Production: In Defence of the Eclectic Theory", *Oxford Bulletin of Economics and Statistics*, 41: 269–296.
19 Teece, D.J. (1986) "Transaction cost economics and the multinational enterprise", *Journal of Economic Behavior and Organization*, 7: 212–245.
20 Inkpen, A.C. (2003) "Strategic Alliances", in A.M. Rugman and T.L. Brewer (eds), *The Oxford Handbook of International Business*, 402–427. Oxford: Oxford University Press.
21 Contractor, F.J. and Lorange, P. (1988) "Why should firms cooperate? The strategy and economics basis for cooperative ventures". In F.J. Contractor and P. Lorange (eds), *Cooperative Strategies in International Business*: 3–30. Lexington, MA: Lexington Books.
22 Child, J., Faulkner, D., and Tallman, S. (2005) *Cooperative Strategy*. Oxford: Oxford University Press.
23 Williamson, O.E. (1991) "Comparative economic organization: the analysis of discrete structural alternatives", *Administrative Sciences Quarterly*, 36: 269–296.
24 Hedlund, G. (1986) "The hypermodern MNC – a heterarchy?", *Human Resource Management*, 25: 9–36.
25 Barham, K. and Heimer, C. (1998) *ABB: The Dancing Giant*. London: Financial Times Pitman.
26 Doz, Y., Williamson, P., and Santos, J. (2001). *The Metanational*. Boston: Harvard Business School Press.
27 Kogut, B. and Zander, U. (1993) "Knowledge of the firm and the evolutionary theory of the multinational corporation", *Journal of International Business Studies*, 24: 625–646.

CHAPTER 8
Entry Strategies for Global Companies

Strategy in Action

In 2008, Grupo Santander became the world's third largest bank measured by profitability (with a profit of almost Euro 9 billion) and its seventh largest measured by market capitalization. It is the largest banking group in the euro area.[1] Santander is highly international in its scope. It runs large retail banking networks in its Iberian home countries of Spain and Portugal and Santander Consumer Finance is a leading player in Germany, Italy, and the Nordic countries as well. Acquisition of Alliance & Leicester and Bradford & Bingley in 2008 has made Santander the third largest bank in the United Kingdom. It is also a leading bank in much of Latin America, to include Brazil, Mexico, and Chile. Its merger with Banco Real in Brazil made it the third largest bank in that country, with more than 3500 branches. Another acquisition, of Sovereign Bank, has given it a strong entry position in the Northeast United States.[2] Besides its multiple national retail banking operations, the Bank also operates in asset management, private banking, insurance, and other financial services on a global basis.

Founded in 1857, Banco Santander operated from the start to finance trade between its home city and Latin America, and 90 years later, after considerable growth through acquisition in Spain, it established its first Latin American regional office in Cuba, which was soon followed by offices in Argentina, Chile, and Mexico and a subsidiary was acquired in Argentina in the early 1960s. Through the 1980s, Banco Santander acquired banks in Germany and Portugal and set up an alliance with the Royal Bank of Scotland. In the 1990s, it increased its activities in Latin America again, and in 2000 consolidated Banespa in Brazil, Grupo Serfin in Mexico, and Banco Santiago of Chile into its region-leading network of retail banking. In 2003, the focus shifted back to Europe as the Grupo set up Santander Consumer Bank through acquisitions in Germany, Italy, and Spain. Consumer Finance now has operations in 12 Western and Eastern European countries, the US, and Chile. Its 2004 takeover of Abbey National, the sixth largest bank in England, generated considerable consternation in that country, and its 2005 partial acquisition of Sovereign gave the group a strong position in the United States.[3]

The crash of the world economy in 2008–09 was accompanied by an equally resounding crash of the world financial system, giving notice, if any were needed, that financial services is a global industry. Banco Santander is one of the leading firms in both taking advantage of this development and in driving it forward. While British, American, and Brazilian interests have been surprised by the aggressive inroads of a bank from a provincial town in a smaller European country, Santander has shown itself to be an increasingly powerful force in global banking. It is also one that gives every appearance of strong management. Despite the appetite for risk shown in its aggressive growth through acquisition in Europe and Latin America, not to mention smaller but important presences in the US and recently Japan, Santander was largely unscathed by the collapse of the market for derivatives of the US sub-prime mortgage industry. Indeed, the group was able to take advantage of mortgage-market and auto financing-based weaknesses of Sovereign Bank to purchase the remaining 75% of its equity in late 2008. As a result, it is sitting on a strong capital base bolstered by one of the largest retail banking networks in the world, with over 10 000 branches worldwide.

Santander has taken its model of strong retail banking to each of its markets, bringing large financial resources and a successful management model to play. So far, none of its mergers or acquisitions has been threatened significantly even in the current down market. Maintaining a focus on customer needs and capital discipline, channeled through a multidomestic model that gives a strong role to local managers to make decisions based on local market knowledge, but within a global vision, has been hugely successful for Grupo Santander. They have used branch banking to support trade, set up local branches in major financial centers to support their private banking and consumer finance operations, and alliances to more actively enter local banking. However, their major means of expansion, domestically, regionally, and globally, has been through acquisition, whether gradually through partial ownership and eventual expansion, or directly through tenders; acquisitions have been the primary means of market entry in Grupo Santander's run to the top of its industry. With its apparent strength during the current downturn, Santander seems poised for continued expansion in North America and possibly Asia, where it has small interests and minor recent actions. Acquisition, which offers quick market position, avoids the need to fight for market share, and allows Santander to impose its successful formula on the new subsidiary, seems to offer a tested route to growth in this industry – one that has suddenly emerged as the prototype for globalization in the service sector, a combination considered impossible until recently.

International strategy in this era of intensive communication, global markets, expensive technology, and falling barriers to trade and investment seems to be all about the connections between markets and the ability of firms to leverage strengths in one place to gain advantage in another. Nevertheless, expanding MNEs still must enter local markets one at a time – even if the strategic objective is to incorporate the new country or region into the larger global network. Entry decisions continue to be critical decisions. Customers are still parts of regional, national, and subnational markets. Production may be dispersed, but still takes place in individual locations with specific characteristics. Locally unique customs, skills, work habits, and regulations, laws, taxes and other environmental inputs give each place a unique set of possibilities whether as a market or as a part of the firm's value-added chain. This chapter discusses the influences that drive to choose one location and form of entry over others and then follows with a discussion of the various possibilities that exist in pursuing a chosen strategy.

Entry Drivers

There are four major forces that drive the entry decisions of the multinational firm, as we see in Figure 8.1. Some of these have been discussed previously in this volume, others have not, but are

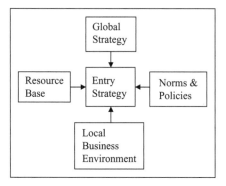

Figure 8.1 The forces driving national entry strategy.

issues typically addressed in great detail in introductory classes on international business that focus on the environment of international business and of individual national markets around the world. The first consideration – at least for a book focused on international strategy – is the overall strategy of the multinational firm. Any market entry decision should be tied to a distinct strategic purpose, whether as an independent market in a multidomestic strategy, as an offshore production location for a cost-driven global strategy, or as a site for unique research and development embedded in the local economy as part of an integrated transnational strategy. Firms should beware "filling blank spaces in the map" and other such unstudied approaches to investment. Market entry involves costs, both real and opportunity, that can be or become very large over time, and should never be a casual choice.

The second consideration, related to but distinct from global strategy, is the norms and policies of the firm. By this, I mean those organizational characteristics that persist over time, often as part of the firm's core identity, as opposed to strategic decisions that are tailored to a particular environment, even when looking at strategy on a grand scale. Corporate commitments to employee rights, to union membership, to the advancement of women within the company are all part of this. Corporate policies toward bribery and other forms of corrupt dealings with local authorities may be critical in some locations. Environmental ethics, community involvement and other concerns of corporate social responsibility distinguish one firm from another and may give an MNE reason to choose one location over another.

Third, corporate management must consider the resources and capabilities of the company. As we have seen, such assets are critical to selecting a corporate international strategy, but they are also important to specific entry decisions for a couple of reasons. To begin, the MNC must have, or have access to, the needed capital to make the investment – and must be able to accept the level of risk entailed by any one investment. Then, the company should consider how effectively its human and organizational assets can be employed in the new market. Do our managers have experience in similar situations, or is this a new and somewhat unique place for us? Will our strategic assets be applicable in this new market, or is a radically different level of economic development or intellectual property protection or consumer tastes going to force us to find new sources of advantage? Not every place is equally resonant with the core competencies and products of even the most powerful MNE.

Finally, the MNE must consider the local macro-environment – natural and man-made comparative advantage, economic development, technological advancement, political stability, regional trade agreements, home-host government issues, local rule of law, and language, customs, values, time sense, and the other attributes of national culture and institutions. Of course, we looked at the overall environment of international strategy in Chapter 3, but now the focus must shift to the details, the daily events and small decisions that will make local customers either like or hate our products, local employees either work hard or create difficulties that can impact global production networks, local authorities work with us or seek to take advantage of us at every turn. The entry strategy must fit all of these constraints and influences as well as be designed to take advantage of every opportunity that arises if the MNE truly expects to earn a desirable return on investment anywhere.

The influence of global strategy – why are we doing this?

The likelihood of success for a strategic move into any new national market – or into a local part of a larger national market – is much increased if the parent MNE has a clear understanding of how that entry move is related to the larger strategy of the corporation. This is as true of the decision to export to a new market as it is of the decision to create a subsidiary with production facilities, distribution, and so forth – though perhaps less expensive and risky. It is also as true of decisions to enter markets or to take on offshore partnerships as exploratory moves or as real options on a potentially important location as it is of decisions to commit major resources to a large acquisition or to building a major facility. Again, the point is to understand how the new move is intended to fit with the existing firm strategy and with any new strategic directions.

As an example, Daimler-Benz made several moves into the North American market over the years. For a long time after the end of the World War II, Mercedes Benz automobiles were exported to the United States. With their image of made-in-Germany quality and engineering and the relatively large size of the American luxury car market, this was a reasonable strategy. In the 1990s, though, cycles of currency fluctuation had led to rising and falling sales and market demand for vehicles such as vans, small trucks, and Sports Utility Vehicles had become a large part of the American market. Daimler-Benz decided to use their automotive expertise to build a line of luxury SUVs. While there would be some demand around the world for such vehicles, the US market, with its relatively cheap gasoline, demand for larger cars, and truck-related image benefits, was the obvious key to success. Rather than exposing the success of this major market to exogenous macroeconomic effects, Benz decided to open a greenfield production facility in Alabama in the southeastern US. The vehicles could be marketed as German engineering made in America, the locale was unfriendly to unions despite relatively low wages, and tariffs on auto parts were considerably lower than on completed SUVs. Possible political benefits and marketing possibilities also derived from a production location in the middle of the highest demand area – an entry strategy that appears to be eminently reasonable given that core parts would still be sourced from Germany, offering increasing scale for engines, transmissions, and so forth, and that overall Benz would continue to support its global niche strategy.

Not many years after opening this factory, though, CEO Detlef Schrempf of Daimler-Benz decided on an even larger commitment to the US market with his widely reported merger with (or acquisition of) Chrysler to create DaimlerChrysler in 1998. This decision to enter the US with a major commitment to a new market segment had various justifications with considerable surface validity. Benz could apply its engineering expertise to a mass market line. Chrysler's new-found design skills and new vehicle development expertise could speed the introduction of new Mercedes models. Jeep offered an additional SUV brand name that could complement the M-class at a lower price level. However, the key to most of these synergies was that this merger would respect the complementary competencies of the two firms.

Within a year, as Chrysler top management left the firm and Schrempf was quoted as saying that the "merger" was a maneuver to hide the actual unfriendly acquisition of Chrysler from financial markets, things began to unravel. The two firms quickly began to look just different, not complementary. The Germans began to push Chrysler to change while absorbing little new knowhow into Mercedes Benz. Chrysler's need for new models and additional investment was met by the draining of its multi-billion dollar "war chest" to cover the costs of acquisition. The executives who left turned out to have been the key players in Chrysler's early-1990s turnaround. And overall, Daimler executives still saw themselves as a global high-end niche producer risking their brand equity with a weak, down-market company like Chrysler.

Initial euphoria turned into a long struggle that resulted in a few successes for the old Chrysler – the 300, a new Jeep line – but many underfinanced and poorly conceived models in the face of constant new offerings from other mass producers. At the same time, the Mercedes reputation for quality and engineering began to suffer as top management attention was absorbed by billions of lost equity in the US. Even as the potential for successful joint operations began to rise again after 2005, DaimlerChrysler top management – Dieter Zetleff, who had led the Chrysler division before replacing Schrempf as corporate CEO – decided to divest the remnant of Chrysler in 2007 in order to refocus on Mercedes. While the exact terms and value of this move are not clear, it is clear that Benz will lose most of the money that it invested in the first place. The acquisition, as internal discussions came out, came to look much more like a vanity project – the desire to make Benz one of the big players – rather than a well-thought-out strategy. Chrysler was chosen more because it was affordable (the successful American players, GM, Ford, Toyota, Honda, were bigger than Daimler-Benz's automotive arm) than because it was respected or desirable. And Daimler-Benz neither had nor really was prepared to build a North American, much less global, mass market strategy. While the company's earlier forays into North America seem to have been well considered moves to build on a clear corporate strategy, the Chrysler acquisition has become a classic of executive hubris and over-reaching in the absence of strategic clarity.

To return to the more conceptual, MNEs should understand their own strategies when considering entry. A multidomestic food company might well buy a strong local brand with the intent of broadening its line, accessing more shelf space, perhaps leveraging some technology, all while leaving the acquisition intact, with perhaps a bit of increased efficiency. Contrast this with an acquisition by a globally focused technology company. The new acquisition should offer its own global product line, technology, and brands. Its operations will be combined with the existing network to increase scale and scope advantages for the entire company while offering a new global market opportunity to a possibly newer, smaller, but somehow unique purchase.

In the first case, the local producer will become part of a portfolio of mostly local brands and manufacturers, benefiting on the margin from being part of a larger company – cheaper financing, better marketing, perhaps new products and processes to try. In the latter situation, the entire global network of the MNE will have to adjust to having new R&D, new products, new processes, added productive capacity. The local firm may well find itself losing its independence to become part of an interdependent network. It may begin to market and distribute products from around the world locally, while shifting production to a smaller assortment of products, but providing them to the worldwide network. Diversification and differentiation of facilities within a global network offer potentially large benefits, but also bring the risk that some other part of the system can break and bring down the entire system, with no opportunity for the local firm to respond on its own.

Research suggests that MNEs pursuing globally integrated strategies are more likely to seek whole ownership, whether through greenfield startups or through acquisition, than are firms pursuing multidomestic, country-by-country strategies, which are more likely to take on partners in equity joint ventures.

As we look at the possible means of entering new markets, we see that markets, alliances, acquisitions, and startups are all possible.

However, they all have different value depending on how they fit into the MNE's global plan. Alliances are relatively inexpensive and offer access to the ideas of new partners, but are also likely to be unresponsive to the need for local sacrifice for global benefit, so can be risky as links in a global supply chain. Acquisitions bring instant access and local credibility in multidomestic strategies, but require considerable adjustment if they are part of an integrated network. Startups offer the chance to build in corporate values and focus from the start, but often must fight for market share if they are aimed at the local, rather than global, market. Every entry strategy can be a success, but every one can also be a threat to the multinational parent firm if not chosen carefully with an eye to fit with the overall corporate strategy.

The boundary effects of corporate norms, values, and policies – that's just the way it is

Global strategies have – or should have – significant effects on entry strategies. However, firms do things for reasons other than strategic choices based on assessments of resources and competitive conditions. Over time, all organizations develop ways of behaving under different circumstances. Extrapolating from studies of human behavior, scholars describe organizational cultures and institutions, group norms and values, and organizational policies. These concepts, unlike strategy, represent pre-determined ways of acting under conditions that are yet to occur. Thus, a corporation that has a culture that emphasizes openness with its employees might create an employee-management task force to consider the possibility of plant closings and offshore production in the face of international competition, while other similar companies might be much more secretive.

A variety of influences may impact entry decisions. One prominent example is policies relating to corporate ethics (which would be norms responding to values that are part of a corporate culture – these are closely related constructs) as reflected in the use or non-use of bribery. Less developed markets are often characterized by extremely underpaid public employees and companies routinely face implied or explicit requests for payments. American companies, constrained by Foreign Corrupt Practices Act (FCPA) penalties on corporate officers, tend not to offer bribes themselves, but other home countries are less aggressive in pursuing such practices, and some even offer tax deductions for bribery payments. US firms, of course, have been known to use subsidiaries or partners to handle such transactions in order to gain some distance from the payment (though they remain liable under US law). Other firms, from many countries, have ethical qualms about bribery and offer firm policies against the practice, with severe penalties for wavering executives. Anecdotally, American companies have suffered from host government pressures in trying to enter markets, particularly when pursuing contested acquisitions or partnerships. Other research, though, suggests that MNEs with firm policies are not put at a significant disadvantage.

Companies may also develop polices concerning ownership. While many MNEs use alliances and joint ventures as regular means of entering new markets, others fear the possible opportunism of difficult-to-supervise partners. Chrysler, for instance, a few years after entering China through a partnership with a local firm to produce the Jeep Cherokee through Beijing Jeep, discovered exact copies of the vehicle being sold by the Chinese partner from a plant located only a few miles from their plant. Coca-Cola withdrew from the large and lucrative Indian market in 1977 when faced with a government requirement to take a local partner and to provide its trade secrets, including the formula for Coke, to that partner. Coke chose instead to abandon the large and growing Indian market for more than a decade, until the government changed its policies. Companies that fear the negative consequences of alliances will go to great lengths to seek whole ownership. On the other hand, other firms look to the benefits of alliances and joint ventures and seek partners for entry even when not required to do so.

Likewise, some firms have policies, or at least preferences, for how they enter new markets. Acquisition can be the best decision based on a rational analysis of the situation, but can also be the preferred – or the avoided – option for obtaining whole ownership. Shared equity through joint venture or partial acquisition as opposed to an alliance contract is a choice in the case of entries through co-operative means that can also be based on analysis or on "how we do things around here". Of course, as companies lean toward one means of entry or ownership position or another, managers become more comfortable with their ability to handle some circumstances as opposed to others, and their teams become more competent and experienced with doing things one way, thereby reinforcing preference with competence.

Other aspects of company culture may influence choice of location and entry means. Human resource policies toward diversity, treatment of women or minorities, rates of pay and bonuses, use of full-time versus contract employees, career management, the importance of third country expatriates, and other such issues of personnel management may be at odds with cultural or regulatory demands from some markets, possibly keeping some MNEs out of those markets. Policies concerning the importance of shareholders as opposed to other stakeholders such as employees, communities, customers, suppliers, and so forth may lead to specific choices of partners or investment form, as may the company's perspective on the role of subsidiaries and other affiliates as opposed to the central headquarters in strategic decision-making. Concern for the environment again may complement or conflict with local government policies, and may also lead to disputes with local partners as one side or the other evinces greater concern for profits than conservation. All in all, companies approach entry strategies (and other strategic decisions as well) with preconceived notions about the best ways to accomplish many tasks, and follow these policies and preferences even in the face of contrary rational analysis – there are constraints on the range of possible decisions that vary from firm to firm.

That just can't be done – the limits of corporate resources

Entry strategies reflect corporate strategies and corporate positions as matters of choice. They must also reflect corporate resources, though more often as a matter of limitations – some desirable choices are just not accessible to some MNEs. Of course, resource strengths can also encourage some strategies over others, but this is a matter of wider boundaries, not an absence of constraints. As we saw in the discussion of resources and capabilities as a critical part of strategic decision-making at the corporate level, the strengths and weaknesses in available resource stocks are critical parts of the entry decision. Limited financial resources may limit some firms to smaller or more accessible markets, to alliances instead of whole ownership, or to startups rather than acquisitions. Lack of international experience and of capabilities at analyzing and managing foreign entry may increase perceived risk, taking some markets out of the picture for some firms and leading to conservative approaches for others. Companies without strong strategic assets may have a difficult time in advanced markets – companies with a shortage of complementary assets may need partners to supply needed capabilities to deliver their product effectively to customers. Even firms looking at national entry to support resource-seeking strategies need capabilities in managing distributed production, supply chains, quality, and productivity as well as skills in dealing with foreign locations, partners, and governments.

Studies show that multinational firms tend to be larger firms – the costs and risks of overseas investment are more easily accepted by large companies with deep pockets. However, high tech firms in today's knowledge-intensive industries are finding that they must become involved in both international markets and international production (and not necessarily local production for local markets) in order to compete on an equal basis. For these firms, though, limits on financial resources tend to force alliances – and often contractual alliances. Whether seeking offshore production to support technological advantage or international distribution, the benefits of contracts – limited exposure of technology, specific performance targets, relative ease of changing partners, and low fixed costs – are all favorable to the smaller firm in a fast-changing, technology-dependent industry. On the other hand, large multinationals have a wide range of options when considering international investments. They can use captive offshoring rather than outsourcing production, acquire downstream logistics and distribution systems rather than taking on a partnership, and they have the assets to build and staff a new facility from scratch in a new market when necessary. Hamel and Prahalad offer a strong argument that cross-subsidies between established, profitable markets and new or developing markets are one of the key strengths of large multinational firms.[4] Of course, examples such as the creation of DaimlerChrysler or Wal-Mart's acquisitions in Germany and possibly Britain show that simply having the capital to buy into a market does not mean that is always a good idea.

More important to strategic success in the long run than financial resources – which may limit immediate options, but can be accumulated over time as the firm is successful – are the strategic assets that generate sustained competitive advantage. Two aspects of such resources and capabilities are particularly relevant to entry strategies. First, firms must consider whether or not their strategic firm-specific resources will play in the new market. Most discussions of multinational diversification tend to assume that the assets that have brought a firm sustained advantage in its home market or other international situations will apply in subsequent markets. This is not necessarily the case, though.[5] Brands do not all resonate in every market. As Wal-Mart has found, logistical skills may not bring advantage in markets where other competitors are equally skilled *and* locally aware. Product characteristics do not always carry over, as has been said frequently of products with high cultural content, such as food and drink, clothing, entertainment, and the like. Even technologies may not offer the same advantage in every market, where bad matches between firm-specific skills and local standards in education, infrastructure, and labor availability may blunt the effects of otherwise superior processes, and local institutions may limit the benefits of product technologies that are superior in the overall global market but overkill in some markets. Firms should evaluate in as much detail as possible, to include involving local advisors and conducting surveys and interviews, whether their core strategic resources and capabilities will provide competitive advantage in a potential new market or not. If not, the MNE should give serious consideration to avoiding the market or at the least to seeking local complementary resources to help put their core competencies back on track.

Complementary resources are a major consideration in the application of strategic resources. A variety of scholars have identified situations in which firms in possession of strong technologies, patents, brands, and the like have failed because they lacked product development skills, marketing skills, distribution systems, and other fundamental supporting competencies and were eventually surpassed by companies that did have the support structure and were able to imitate, buy, or bypass the core resource base. In foreign entry, firms often take on local partners to provide such complementary resources. While particularly relevant to smaller firms that cannot afford to build complex, but not profit-generating, systems, such considerations may be equally important to larger firms that do not wish to over-commit to an uncertain market, or that find the sorts of political and cultural connections that local partners possess difficult to develop from the outside. This situation may be seen as part of the "international alliances as real options" approach, in that multinationals can see how their core competencies play in a market without large and unrecoverable local investment by engaging partners. Failure is relatively inexpensive and success can be followed by either formalizing the partnership or internalizing the partner's role. Of course, firms that already have a position in a market with one product will typically leverage these existing assets to support subsequent investments.

The second area in which the capabilities of the firm are critical is in managing international investment. Firms that have developed significant skills at coordinating networks of internationally dispersed affiliates have great advantage in entering any new country, whether seeking a new market or looking for a new production location. At the same time, firms that have developed capabilities at particular entry modes will tend to be more successful in using those forms. Much research shows that experience at using acquisitions or alliances is the most consistent predictor of subsequent success in using these same entry modes. Research by Kale, Dyer, and Singh further shows that companies that have developed specific units to manage alliances are even more successful than equally experienced firms that have not formalized their processes within the organization.[6] As I suggested earlier, experience – and success – at using a particular entry mode tend to lead to a policy of using this mode and to strategic decisions predicated on the idea that an alliance, an acquisition, a joint venture would be the way to go, even before the details of any decision are clear. In much the same way, experience and institutions aimed at coordinating an international network of subsidiaries can be leveraged to provide support, both financial and substantive, to new affiliates. Knowing how to enter a market or set up a new facility, how to bring that market or facility "on line" in the firm, and how to move from startup to profitability has as much impact on the eventual success of an entry strategy as the availability of relevant technical assets.

Local conditions – what are we getting into?

The fourth force, and the one most explicitly international in scope, is the effect of the local environment. This is a very large issue, one which is the essence of courses on the environment of international business, and one which can only receive relatively superficial treatment here. This is the location effect, the critical difference between strategy and international strategy. The other three forces affecting entry strategies really must be considered in any expansion – how does this fit our overall strategy, does it fit our policies and objectives, and do we have the necessary resources to make this strategic move? However, domestic firms give relatively little consideration to the differences between locations, other than perhaps tax incentives, when considering a new site. This is not to say that regional differences in a large country such as the US do not matter, but only to say that they seldom are a major concern. Entry into a new foreign market, though, puts such issues front and center.

Locational or contextual factors fit in one of two major categories – the international and the local. International issues are those parts of the international environment of business that separate or connect the potential host market to the rest of the world system. A major consideration is the state of the relationship between the MNE's parent country and the host country. In 2007, political relationships between the US and China are relatively stable, if a bit wary, and American companies are investing widely in China. On the other hand, the near-cold war political relationship between the US and Iran makes any investment by American companies in what used to be a popular site for FDI very unlikely. Political ties can be augmented by cultural ties or differences. We see that previous colonial powers often maintain close political and economic ties to their ex-colonies – Britain in India, France in West Africa, the US in the Philippines – giving an edge to companies that can exploit these ties. In other situations, cultural clashes (and political efforts to inflame and encourage them) can hurt market potential and threaten productive investment, as we see today with American oil companies in Venezuela or Western investment in parts of Indonesia where Islamic fundamentalism is on the rise.

Membership of the host country in international institutions can have an effect as well. China has become a much more attractive site for investment from industrial nations since gaining entry to the World Trade Organization. Investments in infrastructure are much more likely if the International Monetary Fund is working with the local government or the World Bank is helping in financing the project. All these connections serve to legitimize the host government and to provide assurances that it will honor commitments as part of a bigger picture. Regional ties can open the way for investment within the boundaries of a free trade area while limiting imports and investment from outside. The European Union continues to restrict external economic interests in the EU in general, but also in the case of individual member countries. Thus, the European Commission on Competition effectively stopped General Electric's acquisition of Honeywell over concerns about monopoly in the European market, even after US authorities cleared the takeover. Japanese auto manufacturers continue to face limits on imports to Western Europe and difficulties in setting up production inside EU boundaries. Companies from the more developed members, on the other hand, have virtually free (and usually well-subsidized) access to new member states that are emerging from the old Soviet sphere.

However, most locational concerns are aimed at local political, economic, regulatory, technological, and cultural considerations. *Political influences* on investment are rampant, even between states in the US. In developing nations, where the political and economic spheres are virtually identical, investment is impossible without political connections. Regulations appear to be written as much to force MNCs to engage with the political as to truly protect the people and the environment from exploitation. Corruption in political institutions can lead to great difficulty in getting needed permits and licenses and to pressures to pay bribes or offer kickbacks to local officials in order to overcome these difficulties. Tax incentives, particularly for large projects, are typically negotiated on a project basis, and political influence can lead to much more generous terms. Pressures to bring in politically connected, if corrupt and incompetent, local individuals and companies as partners in an investment can be extreme. Does having the younger brother of the prime minister on the board of the subsidiary constitute a bribe? Can he harm the company by influencing decisions or can he be sidelined? Can we operate at all if we say "no"? Will future harassment make the annoyance of dealing with this person seem the better option? These sorts of questions applied to a constantly evolving political scene are quite typical of investments in most emerging markets – and in many (even most) developed countries as well. Money and politics are inseparable, and investment can bring much money into a country.

Economic conditions vary considerably from location to location and have profound effects on both market potential and upstream investment. Goods that might be targeted at a mass consumer market in developed countries are going to be affordable only to a relatively small upper-middle class niche in developing markets. Other products which might have no real market at all in the developed world will find wide acceptance. C.K. Prahalad and others describe the potentially vast market for properly packaged, sized, and promoted goods among the billions of people living near or below the poverty line across Asia, Africa, and South America.[7] However, these potential customers cannot afford consumption styles that are common even among poorer consumers in the developed West. Single-use packaging, distribution to the most distant villages, provision of ancillary services, or micro-credit are but examples of adaptations needed to provide affordable offerings to these individuals. On the other hand, the economic elite in these same countries are often wealthier than the majority of the well-off in richer countries and regularly consume internationally recognized luxury goods. MNCs must be very aware of the size and accessibility of their target market in different regions and countries around the world, or they will be left wondering just why positive consumer responses to their products do not result in sustainable levels of sales.

In the same manner, economic differences impact productive activities in different regions. In the first place, the potential for local consumption may be greater in some locations than others. More importantly, though, the relative prices of factors of production and the educational levels of available workers can result in substantive differences in the economic viability of production processes. Production of goods that would be highly automated in the United States might be more efficiently accomplished with more labor-intensive processes in China or Vietnam. Even in locations such as Eastern Europe, where workers are almost as skilled as in the West, things like less developed infrastructure, less access to raw materials, limits to public communication means, poor public health and retirement systems, and so forth may create difficulties in unexpected areas even while lower cost skilled labor makes manufacturing in Hungary or the Czech Republic seem very attractive.

Regulatory and legal systems likewise vary considerably around the world. The emerging legal institutions in much of the developing world make the "rule of law" much less deterministic and predictable than in the West. Consumer and environmental protection are often of less concern than economic development, and we see stories of food products made with industrial poisons or air quality so poor that high percentages of the populations in parts of China are literally dying from pollution. Environmentally hazardous waste from Europe has been dumped in Africa, agricultural chemicals that are banned in the US are still used regularly in Latin America, and illegal settlements around dangerous facilities have contributed to high levels of casualties in tragedies such as the Union Carbide chemical spill at Bhopal in India. Laws are not in place, regulators are uninterested and corrupt, and the police do not have the means to enforce those laws and regulations that are on the books. This can offer opportunities for MNCs, particularly those with less concern for non-economic issues, but can also present risks due to uncertainties about regulation and enforcement. What is permitted today may not be permitted tomorrow, or may suddenly require remuneration that can run afoul of the FCPA in the US. Weak legal and regulatory regimes can be enticing to companies that feel over-regulated at home, but can also turn out to be fools' paradises with no certainties at all.

Even in the developed world, regulatory systems vary and can come into conflict. The WTO's dispute resolution mechanisms stay busy over a variety of trade concerns. Not long ago, American antitrust authorities were considered to be the most aggressive in the world, but since the Maastricht Treaty came into effect, the European Commission on Competition has become a serious obstacle to mergers and acquisitions among major multinationals doing business in the EU. I have already mentioned the collapse of the GE effort to acquire Honeywell – approved in the US, but rejected by the European Commission, and turning Jack Welch's strategic swansong into a debacle. American firms setting up subsidiaries in Germany find that they must bring union representation onto their supervising boards as a matter of law. In much of Western Europe, worker protection has turned labor into a fixed, rather than variable, cost. Pharmaceutical products must be separately tested and approved in the US, Europe, and other developed countries. The list goes on – the advantage of developed world laws and regulations is that they are typically clear and reasonably well enforced, with much less political influence involved than in the developing countries (though political interference in legal matters is an issue everywhere), but they are also considerably more restrictive and offer more protection to other interest groups at the expense of business interests.

Technological awareness runs in parallel to economic development. Consumers in many countries do not have access to technologies that are common in the developed world. Again, some parts of the population in India are as competent with technology as in the US or Europe, but large percentages of the Indian people have no access to technology, whether tractors for farm work, televisions for entertainment, or computers for communication and information access. These people, a huge population around the world, cannot use technology-intensive consumer goods, and also do not have the skills and awareness to work with technology in production of goods and services. Uncertain supplies of electricity make the use of IT in retail, transportation, and communication systems uncertain at best and impossible in many situations, so that the efficiencies that companies have come to expect at home are simply not available in many other locations. This may affect the mix of goods in a Wal-Mart store in Mexico or China, the real productivity of factories in Vietnam, or the potential of local product development in many areas.

Finally, *cultural differences* from place to place can be very large, but even small differences can have important effects on the impact of product characteristics, worker sensibilities, and consumer responses. Culture is a vast subject with a huge literature of its own, and cross-cultural studies exist as an entire separate branch of international business scholarship. I am not going to even attempt to offer a comprehensive look at the impact of cultural differences on international business strategy. Language, religion, family, nationhood, time awareness, individualism, needs for achievement, willingness to sacrifice for the future or for family, and a vast array of other issues vary from place to place in large and obvious ways, but also in what seem to be minute details – but ones that matter very much.

As Americans living in England, my own family members discovered quickly the truth of the aphorism that these were "two countries separated by a common language". In everyday life we constantly found that a few words here and there led to profound misunderstandings, that our expectations of what was important in relationships were considerably different from those of "the Brits", and that driving around took quite a lot more attention than at home. Individuals saw their relationship to their country differently. Patriotism is considered something to be hidden if not suspected, the churches in every village are empty, religion is closely tied to the more archaic parts of the state, and striving for financial success is widely disparaged – Margaret Thatcher notwithstanding, the nanny state is alive and well, and a strong "Bolshie" sentiment runs through much of the population, both working class and educated elite. Given these and many other such observations from a personal level, we can see how cultural differences even between two very similar countries require MNCs to carefully consider how their products should be presented, what their customers will expect, and how their local employees will react to their management methods before casually entering any country.

Entry Strategies

Well, once all the driving concerns of entry strategies have been given due consideration, once we know what we are trying to do, how that fits with our self-image, what our resource constraints and possibilities are, and how the locals will respond to our company and products, what are our options for entering foreign markets? Entries can be executed by new entry into a market, cooperation with an existing participant, or acquisition of that local firm. Organizational governance methods run the gamut from pure market transactions such as licensing or exporting through extended contractual arrangements to whole ownership. Over time, as well, market position changes and strategic approaches change as well – success often results in increased commitment, while inadequate returns can result in reduction of investment or even exit from the market altogether.

Market strategies

Market entry does not require direct investment. Many product and service firms enter foreign markets through *exports from their home market*. Exporting through local distributors in the host market requires relatively small commitments of resources, from capital to management time and attention. If the strategic objective of the entry is to sell in that host market, exports may well satisfy demand while improving utilization rates of production facilities at home and reducing fixed costs per unit in all markets. Exports with little adaptation also permit the firm (which may well not meet any definition of multinationalism while still producing significant income from foreign markets) to maintain its corporate policies with little concern. Local conditions, however, may have major impacts on export strategies. At times, the core competencies developed in the home market may generate products that are equally popular abroad – jet engines, luxury goods, market research, or blue jeans may find natural market niches with no adaptation. However, products that may find a mass market in industrial nations are often luxury or occasional goods in the developing world – people with serious concerns for feeding and sheltering their families may not be ready to buy large quantities of packaged goods, personal care products, or sweets.

An alternative to exports that still minimizes investment in foreign markets is licensing. Companies may be able sell their knowhow directly to foreign customers rather than embodied in goods and services. Companies with unique technologies can license patents to foreign manufacturers and capture the value added from these technologies through royalties and upfront payments. Brands can be licensed as well, with control ranging from simple permission to detailed specifications for design and application. Franchising services brings brand strength and exceptional systems to service providers. Simple licensing, though, often has limits. Unexpected demand may mean that the licensor leaves money on the table, either by missing economies of scale and scope, or through inadequately designed compensation schedules. A licensee with limited skills may either misapply the licensed intellectual property or may fail to adapt (or be prevented from adapting) a "near miss" product to locally unique demand. Franchisees may fail to follow their exact procedures without expensive monitoring and oversight. Particularly incompetent use of copyrights, patents, or trademarks may result in harm to the original brand and company, particularly with the rapid globalization of information in today's world.

Cooperative entry strategies

Market strategies can quickly morph into cooperative strategies as local distributors, licensees, and franchisees sign extended contracts, adapt their activities to the needs of the product, and press the provider to adapt its intellectual property or export goods to the host market. Contractor and Lorange in 1988 provided a list of cooperative strategies arranged in order of increasing commitment – ranging from technical training agreements through licensing and franchising to equity joint ventures – that is still instructive and widely reproduced.[8] On the market-like end of the continuum, we see relationships such as startup contracts and management contracts that are cooperative primarily in the sense that they extend over time, eliminating market incentives after the initial deal is signed. These contracts are intended to provide tacit knowledge of technical and managerial skills to customers, rather than simply offering products or summaries of explicit knowledge. Often, skilled employees are sent abroad for the period of the contract. The customer commits to a particular approach to solving a problem and anticipates adapting its processes. The provider may not adapt its overall approach, but as its employees work with local personnel, the details of any system are likely to be modified to local conditions and cultures – and particularly good new ideas should feed back to the parent company.

At a somewhat greater level of commitment to shared activities, multinational firms may take on local partners through contracts to handle activities with a strong local component, such as marketing, sales, distribution, and service. Local partners can also provide manufacturing facilities, particularly important in developing markets where production costs must be kept as low as possible to compete. Multinational firms that bring intellectual property resources to foreign markets find that many of the activities that surround turning that intellectual content into products can be turned over to partners, so long as the core technologies are protected and the quality of other activities is maintained. These needs can be handled through contracts or through equity sharing, whether partial acquisition or a joint venture.

Cooperative strategies also work in the case of asset-seeking investments in search of offshore production, product development, or information processing. Partners can run contract manufacturing facilities, as is the norm in the case of the sport shoe industry, call centers and help desks for computer assemblers and software companies, outsourced personnel and payroll activities, and the like. Either well written contracts or shared equity can work to minimize intentional opportunism or cheating, and local management has many advantages for running offshore operations compared to culturally and institutionally ignorant foreigners.

Contracts have the advantages of being relatively narrowly defined (typically calling for very specific asset-sharing, and limiting access of the partners to other knowledge), easy to terminate (and therefore relatively easy to set up), and low cost in terms of capital, management time, and opportunity. However, unless the contract is carefully drawn, partners may see few practical reasons not to seek additional knowledge, to abandon one partner for another offering a better deal, to shift assets and effort away from the alliance when convenient, and otherwise act opportunistically. Equity joint ventures are proclaimed to counteract these tendencies by eliminating direct income to the partners in favor of dividends from their equity shares. Partners then should commit to maximizing the performance of the joint venture in order to maximize the joint payoff. However, cheating is still possible. Local partners can drain off technical designs, process knowledge, and trained workers to their own facilities, eliminating the need to share income while competing directly with their own JV. As mentioned previously, Chrysler found its partner in Beijing Jeep producing exact duplicates, using actual plans and designs from Jeep. This scenario has been played out many times in China and other developing countries. The threat of losses or reduced income from the JV are more than offset by the ability to misappropriate intellectual content. General managers often fear equity participations because they feel that common ownership makes limiting access to information difficult as compared to a specifically delineated contractual venture. In addition, organizing an entire new firm, as is the case for a joint venture, is a relatively involved process compared to a simple contract and may absorb a relatively large cadre of workers on a full-time basis. As firms have developed experience with alliance forms and as communication technology has made sharing information easier, contractual alliances are becoming ever more popular.

Compared to simple market transactions, alliances and JVs make for co-specialization, by which the partners become more efficient and effective in the marketplace through adapting their plant and processes to each other. Despite the chances for short-term gain through cheating, partners are often straightforward with each other in the name of long-term gains. Compared to the next option, that of full acquisition, alliance forms bring together only needed assets, allow the partners to pursue other business with other assets, are much less costly, and involve many fewer managerial opportunity costs.

Entry through acquisition

Acquisition, like alliance, allows the multinational to access the resources and capabilities of local incumbent firms (or even those
of local subsidiaries of other MNCs). However, acquisition brings
all these assets inside the acquiring firm. Internalization gives top
management a free hand with deploying assets, particularly including moving them to other locations. An acquisition of a uniquely
skilled local competitor would allow that firm to continue to compete locally, but would also allow the MNC to either start exporting
product, or to transfer knowledge, including tacit knowledge, to
other subsidiaries in other markets without having to coordinate
with a possibly resistant partner. If the focus is on the local market,
acquisition means that the MNC's strategy will not be subject to
interference or modification by a partner with possibly different objectives. Stories abound of local partners in China, for instance, that
are interested in immediate profit acting against the best interest of
a foreign partner's growth strategy.

Also, when the MNC plans to bring its unique capabilities or resources (production skills, patents, trademarks, brands) into the local
market, alliances mean that the local partner retains the potential to
misappropriate these assets to its own uses. Again, emerging markets seem particularly vulnerable to such opportunism, with China
leading the way in piracy of intellectual property. Stories of manufacturing partners producing identical goods on the side, using trademarks on counterfeit goods, or taking proprietary technology for
use outside the alliance are common. Despite many promises and
increasing real efforts on the part of the local authorities to end
such practices, all evidence is that these problems remain. For a
foreign firm interested in such markets and in need of local capabilities in sales, distribution, manufacturing, and so forth, acquisition
removes the possibility of partner malfeasance. On a less ominous
note, acquisition makes matching local strategy to global strategy
less complicated – without an independent partner's needs to be
considered, the MNC can fine tune its strategic instruments.

As compared to a greenfield startup, an acquisition offers faster
market coverage. Nationwide distribution takes time to develop, and
can give competitors time to respond once a foreign firm enters
the market in a small way. Local activities can also be uncertain
when started from scratch – it is often hard to tell exactly how local

hires will respond to a foreign organization, with unique policies, systems, and strategies. An acquisition can leave existing structures in place, bringing in only strategic control and new technologies. A startup virtually requires a relatively significant expatriate presence in its early phases, since it initially will have no local employees. Again, this is an expensive and possibly uncertain approach. An acquisition can involve a small expat team, or may even permit control from a distance, with occasional visits and regular reporting and oversight to keep things moving in the right direction. In a crowded marketplace, an acquisition brings immediate market share and at least no increase in competitive pressures. These benefits have made acquisition an increasingly popular alternative for entry, particularly as national governments in more and more countries are removing barriers to foreign acquisition or requirements for local partnering.

On the other hand, acquisitions do have some potential disadvantages. Loss of organizational identity may lead key local personnel to leave the target firm, taking their managerial and technical skills with them, and leaving an expensive hollow shell to the acquirer. Even if they stay, pricing an acquisition can be a problem in any market, but having the sophisticated knowledge of a foreign market, especially of a very different foreign market, that would allow accurate pricing of acquisitions is unlikely unless the acquirer is already in the market – or pays expensive advisors. In emerging markets, major acquisitions may be aimed at government-owned or affiliated firms, creating an unbalanced bargaining relationship that can easily lead to a lack of accurate information and little recourse on the part of the foreign acquirer. Paying too much for an acquisition, or discovering hidden problems, or finding that supposed assets are less than advertised are all problems with acquisition in general, but all are exacerbated in the case of acquiring into foreign markets. Furthermore, even if human assets stay in place, the policies and capabilities of the target firm may be at odds with the requirements of the purchaser. For instance, an American firm buying a local company in a country where bribery is tolerated, or even demanded, can purchase FCPA exposure unless it can change the practices, and likely mindsets, of the local managers. Acquisition brings local knowledge and local practice, but this may not be all good from the perspective of the MNC – and selective change can be problematic.

Entry by startup

The answer to many of the problems of acquisition when whole ownership is desired and permitted is for the foreign multinational to build its own subsidiary from scratch, often starting with a branch office and expanding from there. As with acquisitions, whole ownership eliminates the risks of opportunism and inconsistent objectives that reside in partnerships. Unlike acquisition, greenfield startups avoid having to change entrenched practices and attitudes. As a new management team is assembled from mixed foreign and local individuals, corporate culture can be established as the local norm. Of course, human and other assets will be costly, but market prices are more likely to be established for many individual assets than for a company, so over-paying is less likely. Fears of risking parent company knowledge and other resources are minimal. Given time, a well-integrated subsidiary company can be structured according to all the best practices of the global marketplace.

Of course, this is not an ideal solution. Time is perhaps the greatest concern with startups. Facilities must be bought or built. People must be hired and trained. Distribution systems must be structured. Licenses must be acquired. All the thousands of tasks essential to creating a viable company must be accomplished, often while the firm faces severe competition from local incumbents trying to stop the entry before a larger, stronger MNC can get a solid foothold. Market share must be taken from the incumbent firms, which are likely to resist, reducing income and often pushing profitability well off into the future. Overcoming the need to simply take time to build the company is often expensive – access to existing top talent, immediate access to infrastructure, and avoiding bureaucratic delays are all possible, but at a price, making the acquisition of a complete firm seem much more feasible.

Speeding up some concerns, such as accessing local knowledge in a specific area of endeavor, may just not be possible at any price. Building customer relationships, accessing local knowledge, becoming a trusted member of trade groups and industry clusters, or becoming part of the local social network all involve building an atmosphere of trust at the individual level. Cooperation can be bought, but trust takes time. So extracting all the hoped-for benefits from a local investment, particularly one with objectives beyond simply selling existing products in a local host market, can take considerable time when starting from scratch. Acquisitions and alliances, when established local firms and individuals remain in place, are faster. Despite their disadvantages and risks, this speed is often essential to getting an acceptable payback in an acceptable period of time for the investing firm. At a minimum, the MNC's management must be aware of these tradeoffs, must know which can be overcome through skill or investment, and must understand what issues are deal killers for each possible entry mode.

SUMMARY

Entering a market just because we have not been there before is no longer a rational alternative. Entering a market just because it shares a common border or a common language or has cheap labor are not good reasons, on their own, to enter new national markets, either. The case I have tried to make in this chapter is that various macro and micro forces impinge on the strategy of a multinational firm – or should do so. All the "big picture" corporate strategies discussed in previous chapters are critical to the decision to enter a specific country. However, so are the constraints of nonstrategic company policies and company resources and capabilities. Sometimes a market is simply a place that we don't want to be, or we just don't have the means to be effective, even with a solid partner (and those partners, of course, prefer to look only to the most successful multinationals, leaving the smaller, newer, undercapitalized firms to take their chances with similar local firms). Finally, the macroeconomic, political, regulatory, cultural, social, etc. environments of the local region can ease the entry of a multinational firm or make that entry prohibitively difficult.

Once all of these forces lead to the decision to enter a market, whether regional, national, or local, though, the firm still must decide how to go about that entry. We have seen that this can be entry through the market for knowhow, using licenses; the market for goods or services through exports; through cooperative strategies using contractual alliances, equity joint ventures, partnerships or partial acquisitions; or through wholly-owned subsidiaries, whether newly founded or acquired (and that either from another multinational, from the government in many emerging markets, or on the local equities markets via public offerings or private deals). Then, of course, issues of organizing the local entity, setting up and maintaining functioning systems, hiring (and firing) workers and managers, and the other details of corporate management must be put in place and set to work. However, as important as these items are to making strategy work, they all merit their own books – and are explained in detail by many such works!

Key Points in the Chapter

1 The chapter identifies four key forces driving entry strategies: corporate strategy, policies, resources, and the local and the environmental conditions in the country of the investment.
2 Understanding the company's capabilities and perspectives on foreign markets in general and of a specific market in particular is essential to successful entry strategies.
3 Entry can occur through market means such as licensing and export trade, through cooperative strategies with either local or other multinational partners, through acquisition of an existing firm, or through a greenfield startup. Each has its advantages and disadvantages, with control often traded for speed and cost.

Notes

1 http://en.wikipedia.org/wiki/Banco _Santander
2 http://www.santander.com/csgs/ Satellite?accesibilidad=3&canal =CAccionistas&empr=SAN Corporativo&leng=en_GB& pagename=SANCorporativo/ GSDistribuidora/SC_Index: About the Group.
3 http://www.santander.com/csgs/ Satellite?accesibilidad= 3&canal=CAccionistas&cid= 1146205899430&empr=

SANCorporativo&leng=en_ GB&pagename=SANCorporativo/ Page/SC_ContenedorGeneral: Santander History.
4 Hamel, G. and Prahalad, C.K. (1985) "Do You Really Have a Global Strategy?" *Harvard Business Review*, July/August: 139–148.
5 Tallman, S.B. (1992) "A Strategic Management Perspective on Host Country Structure of Multinational Enterprises", *Journal of Management*, 18(3): 455–471.

6 Kale, P., Dyer, J.H., and Singh, H. (2002) "Alliance Capability, Stock Market Response, and Long Term Success: The Role of the Alliance Function", *Strategic Management Journal*, 23(8): 747–768.

7 Prahalad, C.K. and Hammond, A. (2002) "Serving the World's Poor, Profitably", *Harvard Business Review*, September: 48–57.

8 Contractor, F.J. and Lorange, P. (1988) "Why should firms cooperate? The strategy and economics basis for cooperative ventures", in F.J. Contractor and P. Lorange (eds), *Cooperative Strategies in International Business*: 3–30. Lexington, MA: Lexington Books.

CHAPTER 9

Global Strategy in a Time of Troubles

Strategy in Action

Offshore outsourcing, particularly of high-end business services, is perhaps the big story of the twenty-first century global economy – or at least it will if the current worldwide financial crisis and recession turn out to be cyclical downturns and not a permanent restructuring of the economic world! Indeed, even as demand slumps in most markets and debt financing becomes ever harder to find, moving operations to their most productive location and sourcing them from the most efficient producers may become even more important to multinational corporations. Despite the many advantages of offshoring and outsourcing value-adding activities, though, these decisions add considerable complexity to the organization of MNCs and considerable challenge to their management.

Offshoring production of manufactured goods from the United States and other developed countries to South Korea, Taiwan, and now China and Vietnam is becoming an old story, although one which keeps organized labor greatly concerned about job losses in their home markets. MNCs had also been shifting production to other countries in tandem with market entry, but offshoring is unique in that it moves production and other value-adding operations to foreign locations, while sales remain in the home, or other current, country markets. Which is why the political cry is about moving jobs, but not sales, offshore.

The basic concept of offshoring seems organizationally simple – just move a plant to a lower cost location. Governance models focus on whether to control offshore facilities internally or through out-sourcing arrangements, usually expressed as a make or buy decision. In reality, though, we find that offshoring is leading to extremely complex organizational schemes. The *New York Times* reported in 2007 that while Boeing and Airbus were using subcontractors around the world to make subsystems for their airliners, both were using Indian companies to write complex software for their cockpit systems. At the same time, Eli Lilly outsourced human testing to an Indian pharmaceutical company, but Cisco Systems was setting up wholly-owned Indian operations with the intention of having 20% of its "top talent" in India by 2012.[1] So, we see both outsourced and internalized offshore value-adding operations. Outsourcing may be kept in the home market – giving specialist work to specialists to permit the focal firm to focus on its strengths has been a popular strategy for years. Should a company outsource its business processes to Accenture, though, it might discover that it has inadvertently gone offshore, as the consulting firm bases *its* business process outsourcing operations in India. Indeed it had more employees in India than in the United States by December 2007.[2] On the other hand, if an American aerospace firm looked to Tata Technologies of India for engineering services, it might well discover that it had kept its work *on*shore, since Tata bought Michigan-based Incat International.[3]

Despite the many Indian outsourcers in the information and communication technology sector, to include Genpact, which was spun off by General Electric, IBM had hired some 50 000 or more Indian employees even as it cut its US force by 31 000,[4] and has additional thousands of workers in China. Genpact, on the other hand, has offices in the US and Mexico to be closer to North American customers. Procter & Gamble has sent its IT and HR and office management systems from Cincinnati to outsourcers in Moscow, while outsourcing giant Convergys Co. of Cincinnati offshores its call centers to India.[5] Even smaller US firms are using Indian, Vietnamese, and Chinese outsourcers to perform back-office services or manufacture simple products to tight specifications.[6]

What has been represented as an in-or-out/off-or-on pair of binary decisions hides many subtleties. Outsourcing is usually done through an extended-life alliance contract – even Nike keeps the same shoe manufacturers for years. Offshoring may be to the least expensive location, if the work is simple; to a more expensive site with a more educated workforce, if the work involves intellectual capital; or to a closer, "nearshore" location for work that requires immediate responsiveness. The upshot of all these alternatives is that MNCs are approaching the "network organizations" idealized by academics in the 1990s as complex webs of subsidiaries, affiliates, and alliances based domestically, offshore, and nearshore, with multiple ties to each other and to the global network.

As I said in the introductory chapter, we are shifting gears a bit in this chapter to look at current issues in global strategy in more detail and to consider how global strategy will fare in the face of the current global financial crisis. The big story in international business when I started this book was the rise of emerging markets in Asia, particularly China and India; Eastern Europe and Russia; and South America, particularly Brazil and Mexico. As I write this in early 2009, though, the collapse of credit and demand around the world is creating great uncertainty about the futures of those countries and regions as well as the traditional industrial economies of North America, the European Union, and Japan and of most of the rest of the world. The increasing economic potential of these rising economies gives multinational firms tremendous new opportunities for sourcing and as markets, but the fragility of nascent modern economies embedded in massive populations that exist at a near-subsistence level of poverty offers unique challenges, too.

Possibly the only trend that is almost certain to survive the world-wide economic crash is the explosion of information and communication technology. Sales of computers, cell phones, and televisions, not to mention routers, fiber-optic cables, and satellites will undoubtedly slow, but the demand for more and better information seems to be embedded in a basic human need. How else can we keep track of the collapse of economies, finances, and manufacturing around the world? How else can we know what everyone else thinks about these events – and about the things that distract us today: the winner of American Idol, the latest YouTube video, what Colbert said last night, prices of hotel rooms in Cancun? Industries and companies involved in building, supporting, and filling the information system have great potential for even the near future – even as they struggle to survive today. For strategy in the rest of the international economy, these advances are making global management a real possibility, but also are forcing "24/7" strategic management of companies in industries that do not necessarily move at such a pace. When every twitch in your markets, of your suppliers, and from your regulating bodies is known instantly by investors around the world, even industrial companies that have struggled to think in terms of quarters rather than years must suddenly be prepared for immediate responses to instant change. And the pressures of an economy in recession everywhere only exacerbate the need for communication. Better information, faster decisions, and a global response can give one firm the edge over more deliberate, less flexible opponents in a world of fewer opportunities.

More than ever, multinational strategy is about knowledge strategy, about acquiring, moving, combining and recombining, adapting, and applying key knowhow in global markets rather than being about moving goods and services around. MNCs still move things, but the real value of moving things is about knowing exactly what things, exactly where they need to go, when they need to get there, who wants them and why and how these things will be used ... not to mention the consulting fees for helping the customer to work out all of these fundamental parameters. The companies that specify which piece of equipment is needed, that make that item, that ship that item, that assemble it to other items of equipment, and that apply these finished goods to solve some problem are ever more likely to be independent, as each firm specializes in what it does well and outsources the rest to specialists. At the same time, ICT permits communication among these links in the value-adding chain that is closer, more immediate, more complete than what single firms could manage internally not long ago. As communication and coordination come to substitute economically for command and control over widespread value creation, companies – and particularly multinational companies – are less needed simply to manage linkages. ICT has vast potential to make MNCs more efficient, but it is also creating a world in which they *must* be efficient, to an ever tighter standard, while still dealing with the location-bound parts of the international system – the people and the nations.

Outsourcing, offshoring, the flat world, the wired world, the integrated world, global terrorism, the end of one history and the start of a new one – companies and investors, workers and consumers, governments and management all have to deal with these and a variety of other new concepts, some threatening and some promising and most a bit of both. How does this fast-paced, threatening, intriguing new global business environment affect the topics covered in this book?

The Global Business Environment

That the Global Business Environment (GBE) is going through multiple changes and restructurings is obvious today, though where that environment is heading is much less apparent. The worldwide collapse of the financial system with resulting drying up of credit markets in many countries is at the top of the news every day. The United States is in recession, with rising unemployment, increasing numbers of foreclosures, and many business failures, but interest rates are dropping and some indicators suggest – at least in March 2009 – that markets are starting to function again. At the same time, though, Western Europe has slowed at a faster rate but the European Central Bank is being much more conservative with efforts to create liquidity, and most of the economies (Spain, Ireland, most of Eastern Europe) that have experienced the most growth in the last decade are experiencing dizzying drops today, facing double digit unemployment, threatening governments, and reducing trade dramatically. East and South Asia face similar conditions as export markets in the US, Europe, and Japan dry up. Oil-exporting countries find the price of their primary commodity export priced at only a third of what it was less than a year ago. Aid programs in Africa are suffering. Latin America is experiencing a resurgence of anti-market and anti-democratic movements. Overcapacity conditions worldwide are most obvious in the automobile industry, but apply to many other sectors. More and more, governments are increasing subsidies and tariffs and setting up quotas or blocking imports. Overall the picture is one of a shrinking international marketplace and a fragmenting global economy as policymakers attempt to placate local populist demands.

Competitive Analysis

Must these conditions threaten international strategies? All indicators are that MNCs will be forced to reconsider their strategies, but there seems no reason to run from international markets. Export strategies are likely to become more risky as currency values become more volatile and trade restrictions are put in place. Global production rationalization and foreign production strategies may come under fire for moving jobs away from markets (an old story), and government policies may be expected to put up actual barriers to offshoring and global value chains. Multinational strategies, by which MNCs produce locally, or at least regionally, for local markets are likely to see a resurgence in place of the globalizing strategies of the last 20 years. Companies are coming under increasing pressure to close inefficient facilities and to reduce inventories and other costs in the face of shrinking markets, but may face conditions under which closing a facility in a country forces abandoning the market, rather than importing from a regional plant.

The companies that dominated in a period of cheap credit and burgeoning consumption seem to be suffering the most in a suddenly smaller, slower, tighter world economy. Those that stayed conservative, limiting debt, growing organically, and focusing on risk minimization were ridiculed less than two years ago as hopelessly old fashioned, but suddenly seem prescient. As markets shrink, the fight to maintain or increase share can be vicious, replete with price wars, cost cutting, and other hard-hitting tactics. However, a crisis led by the collapse of credit seems to be leading to bankruptcies due to insufficient debt servicing capacity and an inability to roll over corporate debt – so the most aggressive firms from last year's boom times are finding themselves unable to compete in the marketplace for products as their finances collapse. Competition will be tough worldwide, but financially strong companies are likely to see some of their competition disappear due to financial, rather than product, market limitations.

With the first signs that even this deep downturn will end in time, MNCs must plan for the future. Overreacting to decreased demand and market fragmentation today may leave companies unable to respond if the future brings a sudden, or even a steady, improvement. Consolidation in many industries to reduce capacity, combined with bankruptcies or extreme weakness in firms with solid brands and products but questionable finances, suggests that low equity prices and excess leverage on the part of some companies may well result in a wave of international acquisitions once stronger firms see the first signs of market recovery. Countries with large reserves – China in particular – are in a position to lead such a strategy, and may well emerge from the downturn with much stronger positions in global markets. American and European companies are likely to see

Chinese, Indian, and other emerging market firms offering "white knight" buyouts. How target companies and their national governments respond to these rescues by these particular foreign interests may change the face of the global business environment (GBE), the array of competitors in many industries, and the relative balance of power in the world political system.

Resource Strategies

Firms that own or control unique resources and capabilities are still likely to outperform those firms that do not. The problem in times of sudden change is that the firm-specific resources and capabilities that offered success last year may no longer be working, or may even be leading to problems. I have described FSRCs as built over time through complex processes of action and interaction within the MNC and between the MNC and its many environments. While this path dependency and complexity do offer protection from imitation, they also make sudden change hard to manage. Inertia, administrative heritage, inflexibility – call it what you will, strongly developed FSRCs make changing direction difficult for most firms. The current recession and global financial collapse create classic capability traps. The firms that were best adapted to the rapidly changing, risk-seeking, over confident era of last year seem to be the most likely to fail when credit is unavailable, overpriced resources can find no buyer, markets are drying up, and trust is seen as an anachronism. Firms are trying to rediscover their dusty competencies at cost cutting, consolidating, and tightening their belts. For banks, the failure to invest in high-yield American property-based derivatives had become a symbol of an old-fashioned mentality, but today it seems far-sighted – and probably has left the bank in the hands of its investors rather than the government. In manufacturing, low debt loads and locations that reflect currency values and low factor costs seem to be once again dominant over rapid, debt-financed expansion.

At the same time, companies that survive the initial rounds of market collapse are likely to look for new sources of advantage. Resources that offered differentiated but expensive products may be cut back while efforts to cut costs and provide less expensive alternatives get renewed emphasis. Capabilities for innovation, new product introductions, brand development and other activities related to expanding markets and excess customer spending power are likely to be suppressed in favor of new or recalled skills at inventory management, minor modification, brand extension, international production, and other low cost ways of appealing to newly conservative consumers. Of course, the market for luxury goods and services will survive, but even here pressures to keep costs under control as demand shrinks are going to force companies to find a new balance between cost control and innovative products.

Integrating Global Strategy

Outside the financial sector, firms are struggling to reset their goals and objectives to a smaller market, and possibly one with new and rejuvenated barriers to trade. Sudden bursts of protectionism are appearing in the US, the EU, and various other countries. Populist politics rather than any convictions of real economic benefits seem to be the driving forces behind subsidies for auto makers in the US and France, rising tariffs on food, and quotas for imports. Whatever the cause, though, if the crisis drags on and national governments are forced to act in response to popular pressures, globalization may well be bogged down or even reversed. Survival, as opposed to growth and profitability, will become the primary goal of even more firms around the world, MNCs will start to cut off their riskier, less sustainable investments, and emerging market MNCs may find entry into industrial markets an even greater challenge than earlier.

However, it seems more likely that trade restrictions will be limited and targeted for political benefit without producing a global collapse of trade and investment. The balance of local responsiveness and global efficiency may shift, but even as labor unions and activists call for local manufacturing and consumption, job losses and low prices are driving more Americans, and their counterparts in other countries, to Wal-Mart and other discount outlets that benefit from offshore production. As consumers and companies in the industrialized economies suffer for their borrowing and expensive habits, we see that countries such as China and India, despite some slowing, still have economic growth, and their internationally engaged companies are increasingly strong. Indeed, we may look back on these years as the turning point where concerns for American and Western European firms shifting production to poorer countries turn to recognition that those "poor" suppliers are extending themselves into downstream operations in the industrial world. We may well be less concerned that companies like EDS or Accenture are using Indian IT back-room services and more concerned that their suppliers like Wipro or Infosys have been using these American firms to provide sales and marketing services – and are now integrating downstream. The need to balance local commitment with global efficiency and international learning will still be essential, but may well be the concern of firms that not long ago played very narrow roles in global production.

Structuring for Tough Times

As the balance of economic power shifts – inevitably, if at varying rates of speed – from West to East, North to South, multinational firms will still need to consider how to organize for worldwide markets. Some of these may well be new firms from unexpected home locations, but the issues remain. At the same time, emerging MNCs will enter a world of superior communication and transportation capabilities, and will be less constrained by needs for tight control of operational details than in the past. There is no reason to think that emerging IT giants will fail to apply their core competencies to their own organizations. This suggests that value chains will continue to be de-integrated and geographically separated – if Tata Consulting decides to open major customer service operations in New York and London, it is still likely to keep its processing core activities in India. Low equity prices and greater cash flows for emerging country firms suggest that acquisitions, whole or partial, and alliances with the controlling partner role reversed, may become even more popular means of expansion, and that existing company names and brands will be kept in place. As many major emerging market firms are organized as loosely held conglomerates, with many single-product affiliates, subordinate companies may organize around geographically separated functions rather than the global product divisions so popular among the multiproduct multinationals that have emerged in the industrial world. Global efficiency with a local face has long existed in culturally sensitive manufac-turing, but seems a key strategy for service companies that must ultimately speak directly to customers.

For more diversified firms, the current trend toward networked affiliates, many of which are alliances, joint ventures, and partially owned subsidiaries seems likely to continue and expand. Increas-ingly easy and inexpensive communication limits the opportunity for improper conduct and improves the ability of MNCs to manage the application of their core competencies even without control-ling ownership. The lower capital requirements of alliance structures seem most attractive at a time when capital is scarce. The potential for alliance networks to defuse concerns for global domination by the integrated, monolithic corporations of activists' nightmares may also offer political advantage should continuing economic weakness encourage increasing protest. Looser ties, even if long-term, provide legitimacy for claims of local autonomy, or at least management input and sensitivity.

Thus, the look of global business may change as the current crisis unwinds. Trends toward the separation of ownership and strategic control will likely continue, and the trend to replace control with co-ordination and communication also seems likely to continue, even grow. Networks are less expensive, more flexible, and more diffi-cult to target. So long as continuing communication technology improvements give these networks increasing communication ca-pacity, they seem likely to become increasingly common. At the same time, the location of strategic decision-making will likely shift more toward the emerging world, in response to market growth and global financial trends. The companies and countries with the cash seem likely to exercise the power that comes with solvency to play a larger strategic role, even as dispersed ownership, de-integrated value added, and complex supply chains for goods and services make identifying the ultimate strategic centers ever harder to define and identify.

New Market Entry Strategies

I suggest that the "look" of global business may well change as a consequence of the 2008–09 global economic downturn. I suspect that this change will be reflected in cascading operational changes, to specifically include market entry strategies. For the largest global MNCs, existing markets include virtually every country in the world. New entry seems to be focused more on accessing strategically important resources and on locating value-adding activities where most productive. Reports of IBM, Hewlett-Packard, and Microsoft, not to mention pharmaceutical, ICT, and consulting firms hiring tens of thousands of employees in India and China to pursue research – research for global markets, to include their home markets in the industrial West, not just for local product modification – suggest a changing view of the emerging market countries. Changing corporate strategy, policies, and capabilities together with evolving local and international contexts suggest the need to reevaluate the purpose and means of entering foreign countries – countries, not just markets. MNCs can be expected to have operations in a country aimed at accessing its consumers, while simultaneously operating offshore production centers aimed at both the home country and other foreign markets, regional or global, and perhaps supporting a major research center for a particular product line – one that may not even have a major market in that particular country, at least at the present time. Some of these activities may come under common management, others may report alternatively to country managers, global product managers, and international functional managers. The transnational model of Bartlett & Ghoshal[7] told us that subsidiaries in different countries would have different strategic roles and different structures. The modern world says that different activities within a foreign country are likely to have different strategic roles, different ties to the parent, different reporting, different ownership – the entire lot.

Many of these activities will be set up through cooperative strategies and contractual alliances. Alliances offer fast and inexpensive entry. Modern contracting is solving problems of opportunism and oversight, aided by massive, constant, and instantaneous communication. They offer the potential for adding new or replacement partners relatively easily. They limit the access of partners to critical intellectual property. They have low opportunity cost and high option value. These signs of flexibility and responsiveness to a dynamic and evolving environment suggest that alliances will be highly valued during the current crisis and during the eventual economic recovery. However, it seems equally likely that alliances will become much more important permanent features of the GBE. And even in cases of acquisition or wholly-owned startup, alliance entries are likely to precede these more traditional, more expensive, less responsive – but more controlled and less independent – means of foreign market entry.

SUMMARY

Things are changing – global strategy must change as well, indeed should be leading change. A newly volatile global business environment that looks set to last for at least a few years, newly acquired capabilities for international operations, and siting based on many options, not just cost considerations alone, all suggest that the conventional wisdom of monolithic expansion, ownership of all strategic resources, and carefully controlled market entry is wrong and outdated.

Key Points in the Chapter

1 Offshore outsourcing is a major issue in international strategy today, a source of political controversy, but also a way of controlling costs while maintaining or improving service to customers – but only if done right.

2 The ICT explosion is changing the face of global strategy and multinational organization by fundamentally altering the relative cost structures of offshore operations and different means of organizational control.

3 The difficult worldwide economic situation in 2009 may marginally slow, even reverse, the most apparent face of global strategy; inter-firm, cross-border trade. However, the pressures on MNCs to provide improved products at lower costs will only be exacerbated, which suggests that integrated global strategies tying together networks of subsidiaries and affiliated firms to "globally right source" value-adding activities will only become more important and more widespread.

Notes

1 Giridharadas, A. (2007) "India's edge goes beyond outsourcing", *New York Times*, April 4.

2 Ibid.

3 Engardio, P. (2006) "The future of outsourcing", *Business Week*, January 30. p. 56.

4 Giridharadas, A., n. 1 above.

5 Engardio, P., n. 3 above.

6 Barrett, A. (2009) "Business without borders", *Business Week SmallBiz*, February/March, pp. 34–40.

7 Bartlett, C.A. and Ghoshal, S. (1989) *Managing Across Borders: the Transnational Solution*. New York: The Free Press.

Index

SWOT analysis, concepts 10–14,
  94–9

tacit knowledge
  see also knowledge
  concepts 96–7, 111–12, 151,
    154–61
Taiwan 42, 45–6, 52, 82–3, 123,
  141–3, 152, 193
tariffs 45–6, 69–70, 75–6, 146,
  178, 197
Tata 65, 83, 194, 201–2
taxation 8–9, 45–6, 60–2, 165, 172,
  178–9
teams, concepts 95–9
technologies
  see also information and
    communication technology;
    Internet
  advancements 87–8, 123–5,
    195–6
  concepts 2–4, 5, 11–12, 15,
    19–21, 23–6, 28–30, 31–3, 34,
    36, 37–8, 42–3, 72–83, 87–9,
    100, 117–18, 123–6, 141–3,
    165, 174–5, 180–2, 195–6,
    203–4
  entry strategies 180–2
  semiconductors 23, 53, 54–5,
    75–6, 100, 104, 141–3
technology-searching
  objectives 23–6, 31–3, 37–8,
    110–13
Teece, David 151
terrorism 16, 86, 196–7
Thailand 36, 106
Thatcher, Margaret 181
threats 10–13, 16, 143–4, 193,
  195–7
time of troubles, global strategy
  193–204
total quality management
  91–2, 97
totalitarian states 58–60, 64–6
  see also politics

Toyota 22, 55, 70–1, 74–5, 83,
  91–2, 106, 108–9, 133, 154–5
  see also NUMMI joint venture
Toyota Production System (TPS)
  91–2, 97, 106, 155
trade disputes 58–60, 76–7, 82–3,
  146, 177–80, 197–8
  see also politics
trade theory, concepts 44–68
trading licences 44–6
transactional cost economics
  see also internalization theory
  concepts 125–6, 127–8, 149–53
transnational firms 5, 38, 79–80,
  89, 91–2, 103–16, 121–5,
  134–8, 144–61, 203–4
  see also cross-national
    integration; subsidiaries
  building methods 144–9
  learning issues 79–80, 105, 110,
    111–12, 124–5
trends in the global market 16,
  193–5, 196–7
triple bottom line, concepts 9
TSMC 141–2

UK 1–2, 57–60, 86–7, 98, 101–2,
  106–7, 163–4, 177, 181–2
  banks 163–4
  cultural issues 181–2
  financial services 86–7
  legal structures 60
  perceptions 181–2
  performance studies 106–7
  politics 57–8, 177
  US 181–2
Union Carbide 180
unique resources/capabilities
  see also differentiated. . .;
    firm-specific. . .
  concepts 21–2, 25–6, 37–8, 43–4,
    92–116, 126, 128, 137,
    199–200
  economic rents 22, 99, 102–16,
    127, 137, 159–60